PRAISE

J Is for *Journey to Joy*

"In this down-to-earth and honest reflection of experiences that shaped her life, Dana offers all of us, no matter what stage we find ourselves in, encouragement to press forward with courage into joy. Her winsome walk through the alphabet and her provocative poems and reflection suggestions come together to create a true work of art that will nourish and bless your soul."

~Marilyn Vancil,
Author of *Self to Lose, Self to Find:*
Using the Enneagram to Uncover Your True, God-Gifted Self

"With authenticity, grace, and a pinch of sass, Dana generously invites us into her life and shares the treasures she discovered journeying as a woman, wife, mom, daughter, and follower of Christ. Each theme she tackles in *J Is for Journey to Joy* is meaty and relevant, while also being bitesize enough to consider over your morning coffee. As you read about God's faithfulness amid the challenges of real life, the journal prompts will help you create space to consider how God is speaking to you."

~Libby Chapman,
Spiritual Director

Dana's book is a beautiful glimpse into her journey as a mom of five and as a daughter of God. The chapter structure lends itself to an inviting time of fellowship with God for any woman—and especially for moms of young kids, who have limited time. Dana's honesty and insight into the adventure of following Jesus have inspired me in my own faith journey and will encourage moms in the midst of raising their families.

~Kim Sahlin
Coordinator, MOPS, at University Presbyterian Church

Dana locates the intersection of everyday experiences and the ever-lasting Word of God and weaves them into a beautiful book from A to Z. Her thoughtful, inviting insights and questions welcome the reader to pause, ponder, and prayerfully consider what new joys the Spirit might cultivate in their heart and soul.

As a pastor, church consultant, retreat speaker, and spiritual director, I'll be recommending this book often!

~Rev. Dr. Courtney Grager
Pastor of Connections Marin Covenant Church

In this down-to-earth and honest reflection of experiences that shaped her life, Dana offers all of us, no matter what stage we find ourselves in, encouragement to press forward with courage into joy. Her winsome walk through the alphabet and her provocative poems and reflection suggestions come together to create a true work of art that will nourish and bless your soul. Dana Meier's *J Is for Journey to Joy* is one of the first books that simply yet powerfully encourages and guides readers through the joys and sorrows we naturally encounter in life. Her authentic connection to the powerful insights lovingly doled out from A to Z ring true loud and clear. Each chapter leaves you with a smile, a song in your heart, and questions to reflect on each day you treat yourself to a new letter.

~Brenda Zane
Founder, The Stream Community & Hopestream podcast
Mayo Clinic Certified Health & Wellness Coach

Over the years, Dana cultivated a posture of listening for God's invitations. In *J Is for Journey to Joy*, Dana shares her experience, re-minding us to exercise compassion and grace for ourselves and others. She affirms each woman's worth, inviting us to remember each of us is enough. We are God's beloved. Using poetry, music, and journaling, Dana created a whimsical way for the reader to likewise develop a posture of discerning the next step to take in our evolving journeys. I am thankful Dana chose to be brave and act on God's nudges to share this book with us.

~Kimberly Nollan, PhD
Research Analyst

Reading *J Is for Journey to Joy* is like being invited to Dana Meier's patio table for a gentle, honest conversation among friends. Mile markers in the Christian journey, hers and our own, rise up and bring laughter, embarrassment, illumination, comfort, and hope. Spend a few minutes with this book and you can almost sense the welcoming smell of her coffee and the deep warmth of a friend.

~Rick Bundschuh
Author of *Soul Surfer* and *Deep Like Me*

J Is for
Journey to Joy

An Alphabetical Path
to Authenticity

May your heart be full of Joy! Danameier

J Is for
Journey to Joy

An Alphabetical Path
to Authenticity

DANA L. MEIER

REDEMPTION
PRESS

Published by Redemption Press, PO Box 427, Enumclaw, WA 98022.

Toll-Free (844) 2REDEEM (273-3336)

Redemption Press is honored to present this title in partnership with the author. The views expressed or implied in this work are those of the author. Redemption Press provides our imprint seal representing design excellence, creative content, and high-quality production.

ISBN: 978-1-64645-284-2 (Paperback)
978-1-64645-301-6 (ePub)
978-1-64645-302-3 (Mobi)

Library of Congress Catalog Card Number: 2020916099

For my dear family:

Marv, Danielle, Delaney, Brett, Mallory, and Megan.

With joy, I also include Cooper and Philip, my sons-in-love.

CONTENTS

BONUS LETTERS

ACKNOWLEDGMENTS

SPECIAL THANKS TO MARV, #MR.WONDERFUL. Thank you for your patience as I have struggled to find my voice and use it with grace. Thank you for your ability to lovingly challenge me to be the best possible version of myself. Thank you for your tenderness when we have conflict and work through it together. Thank you for your commitment to me and to our kids. Thank you for being an example of true hospitality and generosity. I feel so lucky to be "living my dream" with you and our growing family. I love you with all my heart!

I am deeply grateful for the many individuals who are part of my story: my family of origin, my husband and kids, Marla Meier Malone, Aunt Marlene, Aunt Glo, and Uncle Bill.

Melissa Aydelott, thanks for being my fellow homeschool mom and for your consistent support and encouragement.

Brenda Zane, thanks for coaching me to start my book.

Delaney Meier, thanks for helping me visualize the format for my book.

Nancy Meier, thanks for cover artwork.

Athena, Andrea, Dori, and Barbara at Redemption Press for believing in my message.

Thanks also to these gifted writers, speakers, and musicians—your works have inspired me on my life journey.

Books by:

Brené Brown: *Braving the Wilderness, Daring Greatly, Rising Strong, The Gifts of Imperfection*

Rick Bundschuh: *Deep Like Me*

Beatrice Chestnut: *The Complete Enneagram*

Ian Morgan Cron and Suzanne Stabile: *The Road Back to You*

Richard Paul Evans: *Mistletoe Inn*

Bob Goff: *Love Does*

Maria Goff: *Love Lives Here*

Jen Hatmaker: *Seven*

Katrina Kennison: *Mitten Strings for God*

Anne Lamott: *Help! Thanks! Wow!*

Madeline L'Engle: *A Wrinkle in Time*

Jan Phillips: *Marry Your Muse*

Richard Rohr: *The Naked Now*

Marilyn Vancil: *Self to Lose - Self to Find*

Susan Verde: *I Am Love*

Podcasts and Lectures:

Graham Cooke

Ian Morgan Cron

Joyce Meyers

Music:

Francesca Battestelli

Casting Crowns

Lauren Daigle

Brandon Heath

J. J. Heller

for KING & COUNTRY

MercyMe

Ingrid Michaelson

Newsboys

Point of Grace

Ryan Stevenson

Switchfoot

Meghan Trainor

Chris Tomlin

Matthew West

PREFACE

THINK OF IT: WE ARE never, ever truly alone. With all the people in our world, there have to be others with similar life experiences to those we have.

I wonder how many of us wish for the ability to encourage our younger selves, erase a few memories, or have a chance to do parts of our lives over.

We all might wonder what we'd do differently if . . .

In my journey to find more joy in my life, I have used this definition to guide me.

> To be authentic, we must cultivate the courage to be imperfect and vulnerable. We have to believe that we are fundamentally worthy of love and acceptance, just as we are. I've learned that there is no better way to invite more grace, gratitude and joy into our lives than by mindfully practicing authenticity. (Brené Brown)

I'd like to share some of my journey of cultivating courage through my twenty-nine years of marriage, twenty-four years of parenting, and fifteen years of homeschooling five uniquely different children in hopes that you will find encouragement, support, validation, and/or relief that someone out there has at least an inkling of understanding and compassion for what you might be going through. For me, cultivating courage comes as I learn more about the strengths and struggles of my personality type. As I become more aware, I am able to catch myself before I slip into old patterns, so that instead I can practice a better response. Cultivating courage is the beginning of becoming a better version of myself. #Authenticity #Joy

I pray that you feel seen and valued as you experience and interact with these pages.

INTRODUCTION

Dear Reader,

How are you? No, really. *How are you?* We live in a busy, yet lonely world and people ask this question all the time. But do they really expect an answer?

Well, I am sincere with my question. We have so many feelings every day that seem so real at the time. I want to remind you that we are not our feelings. We are so much more. You and I might be able to wrap our heads around the idea that we are not our feelings, but they sure do impact us!

I want to share with you this guided journal experience through the alphabet: how I found joy along the path of cultivating authenticity. It can be experienced randomly or as a month-long journey, or even as a semester-long bible study with a small group. You will find topics that have been, and still are, tricky or troublesome for me along my journey. I've also included quotes and Scripture references that have been inspirational to me, as well as journal prompts and a song title that echoes the theme of each chapter. #BecomingTheBestPossibleVersionOfYourself #MyAuthenticSelf

I hope you feel encouraged and inspired as you begin your journey to joy.

Blessings,
Dana

Life begins just outside your comfort zone.
Let the journey begin.

$\mathcal{A}$ IS FOR

AWARENESS

AWARENESS IS A KEY COMPONENT in my ability to cultivate courage. When I am aware of my shortcomings, then I can go forward on my path to becoming my best self.

A season I call "My Emptying" began after seven years of homeschooling, when I woke up to the reality that I couldn't do any more on my own strength. Nothing. Not teaching. Not keeping a house running smoothly, perfectly, peacefully. I had to let go of all my inferior feelings and remember where my strength comes from.

Through counseling and a precious mentorship with my dear aunt, I became aware of my need to work diligently to empty myself of resentment from past disappointments. These exercises in awareness helped me identify and release built-up bitterness. After only a few practice sessions of releasing my anger and bitterness, I was prepared to experience the Holy Spirit in a new way during an extended stay in Hawaii.

In Hawaii I was keenly aware of God's presence as I experienced the spectacular sunrises and sunsets. I felt hemmed into His kingdom. I felt found. I was experiencing grace. Each Sunday, as the pastor, Rick Bundschuh, spoke at Kauai Christian Fellowship, I wept as I felt the Scriptures come alive, and I felt a profound peace and contentment as the Holy Spirit refreshed my heart, reminding me that I was worthy of love—just because.

I wish for you to become aware of this power in your life on your path to cultivate courage to be your best possible self.

My dear sister-in-law loves words like I do. She introduced me to this phrase that has become a mantra that we share: *ancara imparo*—always learning. I am so grateful that I love learning, because life is a constant classroom full of opportunities to learn and grow.

Here is what I have learned about that:

> Each day, I have the opportunity to practice asking for God's help
> to change my Heartache to feelings of Love;
> to change my Self Shame to Compassion for the one who hurt me;
> to change my Disappointment to actions of Grace;
> to change my feelings of Failure to Boldness and Courage.
> (See Brené Brown's manifesto in *Rising Strong*.)

I have learned that self-awareness allows me a better vantage point to the connection between the physical response of my feelings and the intensity of my response. Each day provides a new chance to practice this awareness and practice taking responsibility for my responses.

I have also learned that awareness is the first step on my journey of learning and growing. Ancara impora is my path to awareness. #Authenticity #BecomingMyBestPossibleSelf

Poems/verses that remind me of God's truth:

TENACITY: Firm obstinance; continuance in a course of action in spite of difficulty or opposition.

Tough-minded
Energy;
Not
Afraid;
Certain and
Independent;
Trust
Yourself

Learn and Grow

If I am willing
    I can journey: Learn and Grow
I am Willing!!
    I am on a Journey of learning and growing.

Reflections through music and journaling:

Listen to the song "Holy Spirit" by Francesca Battestelli. It is a great message to ponder as we aspire to live a life of awareness.

I also recommend listening to the Matthew West song "Forgiveness."

What did you gain from the lyrics of these songs?

As a strong-ass woman, are you strong enough for the little girl in you?

Are you aware of your feelings and the responses you have to your feelings?

As you become more aware of your needs, can you practice compassion for yourself?

How can you practice self-awareness to allow yourself a better vantage point to the connection between your physical response and the intensity of your response?

Try asking God for the awareness of who and what needs your attention today.

Closing prayer:

Lord, I pray that You would open my eyes to be aware of areas that I can work on as I progress on my path toward becoming my best possible self. #Authenticity

_____

_____

_____

_____

_____

_____

_____

_____

_____

_____

_____

_____

_____

_____

_____

_____

_____

_____

_____

_____

_____

_____

_____

_____

_____

_____

_____

_____

_____

_____

_____

_____

_____

She wades into discomfort and vulnerability.

 IS FOR

BELONGING

Live in me. Make your home in me just as I do in you.
John 15:4 MSG

I ALWAYS WANTED TO BE A mom. There are dozens of family photos of me holding babies whenever I had the chance. I loved snuggling with them and bouncing them to help them settle down. I cringe to think that my need to nurture was so strong as a young person that I would occasionally pinch the precious baby just to be able to calm it down. Don't judge.

When I was in eighth grade, I was assigned to write an autobiography. I needed to include sections for my past, present, and future. Looking back on what I wrote as a fourteen-year-old, it is amazing to see how God's hand has been leading me *every step of the way* to today. I can honestly say, "I am living my dream!" That being said, I can also honestly say, "It isn't always easy." But seriously, where did I ever get the notion that life would be easy? We are promised trial and testing this side of heaven. My dear aunt has modeled the life-giving practice of looking for all the signs of God and His loving provision this side of heaven. It's been a game changer.

As a mom, I *do* for my family. I do laundry. I do dishes. I do meal planning, grocery shopping, food prep, cooking and cleaning.

I do homework. I do baking. You get the idea. But here's the deal. I love all that. I have dreamed of this life since I was five years old. But to say "It's complicated" is the understatement of the century.

Before my husband and I pulled our kids out of school to homeschool them, my sense of belonging was out of balance. I wanted to stop pretending to fit into a certain norm for our neighborhood. Our lifestyle was not consistent with our values. We chose to start believing that our identity comes from belonging to God's kingdom. We wanted a more abundant life, so as an act of defiance, we defined our own rules for raising our family using God's truths.

My sense of belonging is a key component in the way I interact with the people in my life. I pray that you too can find the sense of belonging available to you when you invite God into your plans.

Here is what I have learned about that:

Our new lifestyle allowed us space for rich relationship building. Some of our life-giving rituals were regular family dinners and attending one another's events. We became willing to give up our individual wants, desires, rights, and freedoms in exchange for time spent together.

There were certainly times when I felt overwhelmed, broken, and dying from the inside out. However, I have learned that my sense of belonging comes when I practice presence with the people closest to me.

As a wife and mom of five children with individual unique needs, I am finally beginning to grasp how deep and wide God's love is for me. I am learning that my unconditional love for my husband and for my children doesn't even come close to the love God has for me (and for you) as his dearly beloved child.

I don't regret the intentional choices we made in our family. Our intentionality has given our children a strong sense of knowing where they belong.

Poems/verses that remind me of God's truth:

DEFIANCE

Determined to
Engage in the Resistance:
Fueled by Love,
Intrigued by
Authenticity and
Navigating
Courageous Living.
Evolving into God's Design.

BELONGING

Believe whose you are.
Engage in self-love and
Love
Others well.
Nothing can separate you from
God's love!
Identify your
Needs and have
Grace for yourself.

See what kind of love the Father has given to us, that we should be called children of God; and so we are. (See 1 John 3:1 MSG.)

Reflections through music and journaling:

In "How You Live," Point of Grace sings about how our sense of belonging comes from a life lived on purpose.

What did you gain from the lyrics of this song?

What areas of your life seem out of balance?

Are you aware of what changes might be needed to have more of a sense of belonging in your life?

Finish this sentence: My sense of belonging comes from_____.

Closing prayer:

Lord, I pray that you would instruct me and teach me in the way I should go. Counsel me and lead me to your loving arms. (See Psalm 32:8.)

_____

_____

_____

_____

_____

_____

_____

_____

_____

_____

_____

_____

_____

A sense of belonging is available to you
when you invite God into your plans.

C IS FOR
CONNECTION

*Is there any place I can go to avoid your spirit? to be out of
your sight? . . . Oh, he even sees me in the dark!*
Psalm 139:7–10 MSG

CONNECTION: THE ENERGY THAT EXISTS between people
when they feel seen, heard, and valued; when they can give and receive without judgment; when they derive mutual sustenance and
strength from the relationship.

Toward the end of our first year of homeschooling, the kids
were nine, seven, five, and twenty months old. My mom was diagnosed with ALS at the same time I was diagnosed with the surprise
pregnancy of baby number five!

My mom had been such a support; she came over several times
a week, as I learned to balance my roles as wife, mom, and teacher.
Now this? *How can I lose my mom, much less be able to raise five kids
without her help?* I wondered.

The next nine months were surreal. Every month the baby grew
in me, my mom lost significant mobility and muscle function. By
the time I delivered my baby, my mom was in a motorized wheelchair and talking was laborious. I knew that the only way we were
going to get through this was with God's grace. We chose to use
Grace as a middle name for our newest blessing as a constant re-

minder that in all circumstances we need that same grace we were leaning on in this moment.

When we have the privilege of time, we can look back and see God's wisdom and sovereignty. I realize now that as my mom was losing her ability to talk, her heart and spirit were still very much alive. Every time we visited, she held baby Grace on her chest and prayed blessings on her and all her children and grandchildren.

In that year of life and death, I said of our homeschooling, "We did not do a lot of book learning, but we learned so much about *life*." We had special visits in Grandma's garden, tea parties with Grandma, days of caring for her, reading to her, and just practicing presence. The world would want me to believe that was not enough. But I know that is a lie. We were making a lasting connection. We all received mutual sustenance and strength from that relationship.

Here is what I have learned about that:

Connections happen when we get curious about people's thoughts, feelings, and actions. I see a flowerpot with three flowers in it. Each stem is part of the cycle of connection: thoughts, feelings, actions. I want to get curious about the beautiful blooms that could grow if I practiced cultivating this cycle.

Poems/verses that remind me of God's truth:

> Don't be afraid for I am with you; Do not be "discouraged" for I am your God; I will strengthen you. I will help you. I will uphold you with my victorious right hand. (Isaiah 41:10 NLT)

I Am Enough

I will face Discomfort and Vulnerability head on;
I will get real with My Baggage;
I will have the courage to Feel the Pain;
I will have the courage to Recognize Shame;
I will have the courage to Recognize Regret;
I will Reach out and Expose my feelings;
I will take learning to new levels.
I may make mistakes, but I am *enough*!
(See Brené Brown's manifesto in *Rising Strong*.)

Reflections through music and journaling:

What does the song "Everybody" by Ingrid Michaelson say to you about your need for connection?

Who or what do you want to connect with?

What do you hope to receive from that connection?

What makes you feel unworthy of connection? Can you give up that lie?

Closing prayer:

Thank you, Lord, for your promise that nothing can ever separate me from your love. (See Romans 8:38–39.)

_____

_____

_____

_____

_____

_____

_____

_____

_____

_____

_____

_____

_____

_____

_____

_____

_____

_____

_____

_____

_____

We are all wildly imperfect in our own gorgeous way.
—Shauna Niequist: Present over Perfect

D IS FOR

DREAM

Commit to the Lord whatever you do [dream],
and he will establish your plan.
Proverbs 16:3 NIV

I HAD AN IDEA: A DREAM. I wanted to try homeschooling and simplify our lives with a major schedule change. With a master's in education and having "retired" from teaching seven years before to be a stay-at-home mom, I wanted to use my gifts and talents in a new, fulfilling way.

It was exhausting to get all four kids up and ready in the morning just to drop off my oldest for second grade. The five-year-old went to afternoon kindergarten, and the three-year-old had preschool only twice a week, so we would often take morning outings to the zoo without our second grader. This was upsetting to all of us. It didn't feel right. When they were all at school, I missed my kids. When they came home, they were so tired, and there wasn't much time before the whole dinner and bedtime routine. We were only two years into this roller-coaster ride called public school, and I wanted off. I was getting nauseous!

There was so much more I wanted for our family. I wanted a more relaxed schedule that would allow learning to happen without so much chaos and stress. I wanted to reprogram our family by sending the message that we do things together. I wanted to enjoy the unique stages that my kids were in. I wanted to capture the natural wonder of learning *with* my kids. I wanted to have more meaningful family time and more influence and impact on our young family.

This quote jumped off the page of my devotional journal at the time, and I don't believe it was a coincidence: "Simplicity is richness: fasting is feasting. Disciplines of abstinence help us to empty ourselves so that we become hungry for new things that really matter" (Jen Hatmaker, *Seven*).

My husband and I agreed to see what God had in mind for us in the way of simplifying our family's activities. We began our journey of homeschooling.

Here is what I have learned about that:

Years later, I wondered sometimes, *Had I wasted time by home-schooling my kids and not going back to work?* This doubting sent me on an accelerated path of learning that led me to Strength-Finders. It revealed my top five strengths as empathy, adaptability, strategic, connectedness, and learner. This was the encouragement and affirmation I needed that I had been using my strengths all along by being a stay-at-home mom. #NothingWasted.

I started claiming verses such as 1 Samuel 16:7 and Deuteronomy 14:2 (see below). Once I let go of baggage about not fitting in, I was freed up to dream about how to share my story.

Poems/verses that remind me of God's truth:

> *I feel like an overdue chrysalis, ready to burst open but unsure of my identity. When I am alone to dream, I feel so alive. I want to be a person of purpose.* (My anguished thoughts during my panic attack season)

There is a part of every living thing that wants to become itself: the tadpole to a frog, the chrysalis into a butterfly, a damaged human into a whole one. That is spirituality. (Ellen Bass)

Dear Daughter of the King,

There are incredible things that need to be done that only you can do.
Your life has a beautiful story to tell.
You can do it! Be brave!
You were never meant to fit in. You were meant to stand out as a light in the darkness.
You were born to shine.
You are loved.
(From a card I was given)

The Lord sees not as people see; The Lord looks at the heart.
(See 1 Samuel 16:7.)

The Lord has chosen you as His treasured possession.
(See Deuteronomy 14:2.)

Reflections through music and journaling

When my fears and doubts get in the way of daring to dream, "The Breakup Song" by Francesca Battestelli reminds me to be bold and brave in my identity as "Daughter of the King."

What did you gain from the lyrics of this song?

What dreams are on your mind?

What fears and doubts are in your way to achieving those dreams?

Copy the letter above and personalize it to be a positive reminder of your potential and God's impression of your purpose in life.

Closing prayer:

Thank You, Lord, that you see my heart. Help me to keep dreaming the dreams you put on my heart.

_____

_____

_____

_____

_____

_____

_____

_____

_____

_____

_____

_____

_____

_____

Dare to dream.

 IS FOR

EMPATHY

Every good and perfect gift is from above, coming down
from the Father of the heavenly lights, who does not
change like shifting shadows.
James 1:17 NIV

WHEN I ENCOUNTER A LACK of empathy and compassion, it leaves me feeling empty and alone. Here are a few definitions to ponder. Try placing each definition in the formula below to make meaning for yourself.

Empathy: to understand and share the feelings of another.
Compassion: sympathetic concern for the suffering of others.
EMPATHY happens after we have practiced COMPASSION:
CONNECTEDNESS happens when we have EMPATHY:
COMPASSION infuses EMPATHY:
EMPATHY leads to CONNECTEDNESS.

As I look back at what felt like a successful day as a mom of several kids, I want to cringe. I put unreasonable pressure on myself. If I were encouraging a young parent today, I would celebrate with them if they could accomplish in one week what I put on myself to accomplish in one day.

Get groceries

Take kids for haircuts

Play with the kids (I actually had to remind myself to do that sometimes)

Call my sister

Organize playroom

Make dinner

Host a playdate for oldest daughter

Give the baby a bath

Sit down and journal (I actually had to remind myself to do that too)

And I wondered what was wrong with me when I was so tired. Was I practicing empathy for myself?

Here is what I have learned about that:

E is also for Enneagram: an ancient typology system that explains nine different core personalities. I have learned through the enneagram that envy robs me of feeling "enough." I tend to replay negative messages in my life. I was not talking to myself as a friend. For years I believed lies that I wasn't worthy of receiving good things until I could get my act together.

I am worthy! You are worthy!

I encourage you to remember that God is our perfect example of empathy and compassion. Lack of empathy for ourselves and others is like a cancer that takes over in our spirit.

Don't doubt your value. Don't run from who you are.
—C. S. Lewis: *Voyage of the Dawn Treader*

Poems/verses that remind me of God's truth:

CANCER

Cancer is that place where I can see that I

Cannot

Always be in the know,

No! It is the place where I

Can always

Engage in the

Race!

My race is

grace and I see in every

face who needs this

grace. It's you, it's me, it's every

face, every

race. Just put the mirror in

place to see the reflection back. It's

grace. Jesus did it for me, did it for you. Every

hurting

face in this

place can show what was done.

If Christ is in you and you are a reflection of

Christ,

then take that mirror all over the place and shine

that

grace to every

face you meet today

and every day

because at this

pace, it's a long

race

. . . and I don't like to lose.

Reflections through music and journaling:

"Love Like This" by Lauren Daigle is such a comfort to me that in God's great empathy, He will always comfort me. He will never leave me alone.

What did you gain from the lyrics of this song?

Who is in need of your compassion and empathy?

Try asking God to bring to mind someone in need of your compassion.

How do you make meaning with the formula above?

Closing prayer:

Lord, help me to turn my doubts about not being enough into prayers. I want to sense Your wholeness come settle me down. Help me remember that I am Your beloved child.

Be strong and courageous. —Joshua 1:8

$\mathscr{F}$ IS FOR

FAVOR

For the Lord God is a Sun and Shield; the Lord bestows
[present] grace and favor and [future] glory (honor, splen-
dor, and heavenly bliss)! No good thing does he withhold
from those who walk uprightly.
Psalm 84:11 AMPC

IT WAS AGAIN IN KAUAI where I started a season of unpack-
ing some of my baggage. With the help of Graham Cooke, Brené
Brown, and of course my loving Parent God, I learned a few things.
In *Rising Strong*, Brené Brown talks about how we have a tendency
to weave these "hidden, false stories" into our lives and they eventually distort who we are and how we relate to others. She calls this
"conspiracy thinking" and believes that it is all about "fear-based,
self-protection and our intolerance for uncertainty." Ick! I didn't
want to keep running my story on repeat and attaching my version
of someone else's "intent."

Graham Cooke had a refreshingly real and compassionate way
of addressing baggage. He suggested, "Mindsets and beliefs about
ourself are baggage." He further described baggage as letting your
worst enemy pack your bags for your vacation and getting to your
tropical paradise just to find out that what was packed was for the

arctic. Cooke challenged me to wonder, *What if I don't have baggage, just luggage that hasn't been unpacked yet?* My luggage is the promises that I have studied in Scripture but have never accessed. I was challenged by this idea. If I give power to that which I focus on, then I want my focus to be in sync with God's ideals.

I took Graham's suggestion to ask God for a life verse. I started digging through the Scriptures and praying for a verse or passage that I could unpack whenever I felt the weight of my baggage. I started with Isaiah 41:10–15, per Graham's permission to borrow one of his verses.

> Fear not, there is nothing to fear, for I am with you: do not look around you in terror and be dismayed, for I am your God, I will strengthen you and harden you to difficulties, yes, I will help you; yes, I will hold you up and retain you with my victorious right hand of righteousness and justice. For I, the Lord your God, will hold your right hand; I am the Lord, who says to you, Fear not; I will help you. Fear not, you worm of Jacob, you people of Israel! I will help you, says the Lord; your Redeemer is the Holy One of Israel. Behold, I will make you to be a new, sharp, threshing instrument, which has teeth: you shall thresh the mountains and beat them small and shall make the hills like chaff.

Here is what I have learned about that:

My greatest fear is to be misunderstood. I felt like something was wrong with me; that I wasn't enough. When I am led by fear, I cannot live in favor. I have come to believe that fear and anxiety are closely linked and have nothing to do with a loving God. I wrote these poems as reminders that I don't need to give into fear. I want to embrace my fears and ask God His opinion about my opinion.

I am finally beginning to better understand how favored I am by God. I challenge you to start believing that you are also greatly favored by God.

Poems/verses that remind me of God's truth:

> *FEAR is the evil twisting of things to appear real.*

False **E**vidence **A**ppearing **R**eal.

Facing My Fears

When Fear threatens and I draw in
Give me strength to own my **Story!**
Give me integrity to stay away from **easy**. Help me be courageous and flee from Sin.
I have been told I am **Defiant** and at times **Too Sensitive! I know with God I am a Giant** and can gain territory if I obey **His Command:**
Being Strong and Courageous—I will go forth with a sieve; to go sort out and face what I want to **Reclaim.**
Time will tell; It's not a Race
I can have the last word: **NOT SHAME!**
Instead of living in fear, I am practicing leaning into and embracing living in Favor—that I am God's favorite. (So are you)

Flowing with
Abundant
Victories:
Obstacles
Reduced!

Reflections through music and journaling:

When I am afraid, "Hello, My Name Is" by Matthew West reminds me that God has favor for me and also for you.

What did you gain from the lyrics of this song?

Write a list of things you are afraid of. Mark it out with a big X.

How is fear lying to you or stealing your happiness?

Closing prayer:

Lord, help me to remember to put my trust in your love and favor for me when I am afraid. (See Psalm 56:3–4.)

_____

_____

_____

_____

_____

_____

_____

_____

_____

_____

_____

_____

We are all God's favorite!

G IS FOR

GRACE

My grace is enough, it's all you need.
My strength comes into its own in your weakness.
2 Corinthians 12:9 MSG

MY OLDEST DAUGHTER PROVIDED ME with one of my earliest examples of how God uses my children to teach me about His love. When she was five, our family included a three-year-old daughter and a one-year-old son. I was not the most balanced or patient person. I was unable to do anything nice for myself, being busy *doing* for my young family. I found myself relying on my five-year-old to be "mommy's little helper," though this was not how she was wired. She needed me to see to her needs, not the other way around.

One day this daughter pushed her strong will on me one too many times, and I was a mad mommy who yelled at her and spanked her in anger. After a big deep breath, I went to my sweet girl and told her I was so sorry and that Mommy had made a mistake, and I asked if she would forgive me? She said, "Mommy, I do forgive. I just don't know why you keep saying sorry for the same thing?"

Ummmmmmm! Gulp!

I told my sweet daughter that because I am human, I often

make selfish choices. I had been unreasonable to expect so much from her and to have lost my temper.

I challenge you to start practicing grace for yourself and receiving grace from God as part of his plan for you.

Here is what I have learned about that:

Here's the deal: I needed to forgive myself and have grace for myself in regard to the story about my daughter. Parenting is hard work, especially for someone like me, who was too prideful to ask for help and unskilled at receiving help. It took me a long time to realize that I wasn't a failure for needing help. I just needed help. Seriously though, again I ask, where did I ever get the notion that life would be easy and I should be able to do it all on my own?

I've heard it said, "Evil cannot create; evil cannot destroy; evil rearranges information and sits back to watch us destroy each other." Truth is powerful! Lies ruin relationships, but lies have limited power. Doubting our identity or value weakens our progress in relationships. Unity can be developed when I am confident in who I am. I needed to turn off the messages I had on repeat and to play a new tape.

I am enough! You are enough! Accept grace.

Poems/verses that remind me of God's truth:

Growing in Grace

Lord,
Take my selfish heart;
my anger and resentment;
my pride and my toxic attitude.
Make me approachable, loving, gracious,
humble, teachable, and joyful.

Don't Mess With Me

I am a force to be reckoned with—I may have a bruised heart, but I am owning my story rather than hiding.

I don't want my baggage to define me by denying things happened. I am practicing leaning into truth—looking it in the eye!

God is the author of *my story*!

Grace is the reminder that we are all
God's **R**edeemed and **A**dored **C**hildren for **E**ver

Reflections through music and journaling:

"Greater" by MercyMe has a rich message about God's grace for us.

What did you gain from the lyrics of this song?

What is something that is really stretching you to grow in grace?

Can you tell yourself, "This is hard right now, but I've got this!"

Are you unable to do anything nice for yourself, being busy *doing* for others? In what ways do you need help? Are you able to ask for help?

How can you forgive yourself and have grace for yourself?

Closing prayer:

Thank You, Lord, that in Your lovingkindness You take us firmly by the hand and lead us into a radical life-change.

It's time to turn off negative messages and start receiving grace.
—Graham Cooke

IS FOR

HOPE

God can do anything, you know—far more than you
could ever imagine or request in your wildest dreams!
He does it not by pushing us around but by working with-
in us, his Spirit deeply and gently within us.
Ephesians 3:20–21 MSG

I CAN'T HELP HAVING NEEDS OR getting my feelings hurt or feeling disappointed, but raising a red flag when I start moving toward frustration can help me stay away from bitterness, resentment, and contempt. According to the Gottman Institute, contempt is the most destructive behavior in relationships. Contempt, simply put, says, "I am better than you. You are lesser than me."

When I feel threatened by contempt, I freeze up and numb out. This numbing has sometimes lasted hours, days, weeks. These are times when I feel like I'm wandering around in the wilderness with no direction and no hope. I am learning to invite God into these times of need. Instead of heading toward contempt, I use prayer like this to reset.

Gracious and loving God,

Please send Your transforming power into my life as I seek to serve You today. Grant me wisdom, courage, grace, and strength to faithfully fulfill the role to which You have called me.

In Christ's name. Amen.

God tells us over and over again in the Bible to not be afraid. Apparently it is human nature to be afraid. God had me where He wanted me to teach me a new lesson about hope. He was reminding me to stop wandering around in the wilderness and to pitch my tent in the "land of hope." I challenge you to start believing that pitching a tent in the land of hope is part of God's plan for you.

Here is what I have learned about that:

As my dear aunt continues to speak hope into my life, she helps me "see" my blinders to the life-giving signs of heaven here on earth and how God is lovingly providing for me. Just as He did for the famous desert wanderers of the Bible, God has been supplying my daily needs (manna), yet I am either grumbling or unaware of the value of his provisions.

> Grace can be the experience of a second wind, when even though what you want is clarity and resolution, what you get is stamina and poignancy and the strength to hang on. Through the most ordinary things, books, for instance, or a postcard, or eyes or hands, life is transformed. (Anne Lamott: *Help Thanks Wow*)

Hope comes when I can recognize and receive grace in new ways.

Poems/verses that remind me of God's truth:

God is a safe place to hide, ready to help when we need him. (Psalm 46:1–2 MSG)

Is anyone crying out for help? God is listening, ready to rescue you. (Psalm 34:17 MSG)

HOPE

Happens when we set goals;
Operate with flexibility and allow other
People to be a part of reaching our goal.
Expecting results and believing in ourselves.

Help me, Lord, to pitch my tent in the land of *hope*:
Healthy **O**ptimism: **P**erseverance; **E**ndurance.

Hope inspires conversations with loved ones—making a way to connect with others. (Susan Verde: *I Am Love*)

Reflections through music and journaling:

The message of hope is found in trusting lyrics like Lauren Daigle sings in "Look Up Child."

What did you gain from the lyrics of this song?

Can you think of one or two friends who need to hear this message today? Sometimes helping others helps us get out of our slump.

Could you rewrite one of these verses or share this song with them?

Have you ever experienced occasional "kinks in the flow" of life-giving aspects in some of your personal relationships?

Can you admit your pride and your self-satisfaction and go to those you want to reconcile with to preserve hope?

Closing prayer:

Thank You, Lord, that You are a safe place to hide and that You are ready and available when I need help. This reality gives me hope.

_____

_____

_____

_____

_____

_____

_____

_____

_____

_____

_____

_____

_____

_____

_____

_____

Hope comes when we can recognize and receive grace
in new ways.

I IS FOR

INTEGRITY

So what do you think? With God on our side like this,
how can we lose?
Romans 8:38–39 MSG

INTEGRITY: THE QUALITY OF BEING honest and having strong moral principles; honesty, virtue, sincerity, unity.

My prayer from day one of our homeschool journey was to receive the Lord's help to keep me calm, fresh, patient, and loving as we learned how to live and learn in the same space. I prayed for organizational help and for a smooth routine to be fleshed out. I practiced prayerfully thanking God every day for the privilege to be with my kids and for his patience with me.

I also prayed for my heart to remain teachable. God gave me this passage as we started homeschooling. Here is what I held on to:

> May all who seek to take my joy be put to confusion.
> May all who seek you, rejoice and be glad in you. (See Psalm 40:14–17.)

I claimed this message many times throughout the year as well-meaning friends and strangers would often question our choice to pull the kids out of school.

By day two of this new lifestyle, I was already tired! But I loved what was happening in our home. It was evident that we were a happy home and we were having fun learning. We were more cohesive in our first two days of homeschooling than we had been in the past four years.

Day three started, and the newness and excitement were gone. The only thing my kids wanted to do was build with Playmobile and LEGO all day. Guess what? I let them! Play is such an important part of learning. My kids were happy, creative, and engaged with each other. My heart was doing backflips.

After five months of this new rhythm of on-task time with our curriculum, outings together, structured and unstructured playtime, our kids were progressing and were happy. I think that is the most relevant report card a parent could ever get!

I was challenged to give up comparing myself to other homeschool moms and other families in our neighborhood. On my path toward authenticity, I no longer needed to use comparison as my measuring stick. It was enough to know that this was the right thing for our family. I challenge you to start believing that integrity is part of God's plan for you.

Integrity, to me, is the consistent cohesion of how I live my life and how I say I live my life.

Here is what I've learned about that:

Martin Luther King Jr. described how "hope and power are interconnected when one uses their abilities to affect change." I believe hope and integrity are connected. Hope happens when I set realistic goals and can figure out how to achieve them. I need to work with diligence and flexibility, and I need to believe in myself. This is not easily done. #Integrity #Authenticity

When faced with questions and doubt, I try not to ask, "Why?" It is an invalid question that makes an invalid of myself—it causes me to assume a victim stance. Instead, I am practicing asking God,

"What does this all mean?"

"What should I do now?"

"What do You want to do for me in this situation?"

God uses challenges so that He can speak tenderly to me about the next part of my growth. This can sometimes be a difficult and lonely journey.

A person of integrity needs to steer clear of *easy* and block out the voice of *shame*.

Perhaps I am finally catching on to what Brené Brown was talking about in her guidepost to wholehearted living. "Cultivate meaningful work versus self-doubt and 'supposed to'" (Brené Brown, *Gifts of Imperfection*).

Poems/verses that remind me of God's truth:

EASY—**E**rases **A**ll that God **S**ays He wants to do for **Y**ou

> "This is supposed to be easy; it's not worth the effort.
> This should be easier; I must not be good enough."
> —Shame (source unknown)

> "I use imperfect people to accomplish my perfect will .
> . . I always have, and I always will."
> —God (source unknown)

> "I am the Lord your God who will take hold of your hand. Do not fear: I will help you." (Isaiah 41:13 NIV)

> "Whether you turn to the right or to the left, your ears will hear a voice behind you, saying, 'This is the way; walk in it.'" (Isaiah 30:21 NIV)

Reflections through music and journaling:

If integrity is staying away from easy, then the song, "It's Your Life" by Francesca Battestelli is a great reminder of living a life consistent with my values.

What thoughts came to you through this song?

Reflect on this verse:

> When you come looking for me, you will find me. Yes, when you get serious about finding me and want it more than anything else, I'll make sure you won't be disappointed. (Jeremiah 29:13 MSG)

What does this verse say to you? Does it inspire you? How? What does integrity mean to you?

Closing prayer:

Lord, be my source of strength to stay away from wanting the easy way. I want to live a life of integrity and bring honor to You.

_____

_____

_____

_____

_____

_____

_____

_____

_____

_____

_____

_____

_____

_____

_____

_____

_____

_____

_____

_____

_____

_____

_____

_____

_____

_____

Cultivate meaningful work versus self-doubt and "supposed to."
—Brené Brown

J IS FOR

JOY

You will show me the path of life; in Your presence is full-ness of Joy; at Your right hand are pleasures forevermore.
Psalm 16:11 NKJV

AS I MENTIONED IN A is for Awareness, I felt a profound peace and contentment as the Holy Spirit cleansed my heart during church in Kauai. This is what I heard the pastor say:

> Lord of all grace, I need your Holy Spirit to fill me with Your life. My flesh profits nothing. Lord, each day I need the power of Your resurrection working in my life. I have no effective power that I can generate on my own. I praise You that these are available through my humble dependence on You.

Shortly after that experience, I had a panic attack. I wondered why, with so much to be thankful for, did I have such a heaviness of despair rather than joy.

During my post-panic attack season, I was reminded that I needed to invite God into what I was doing *each day*. God kept putting the pieces of my life together like a giant puzzle. I didn't know what it would look like—I couldn't see clearly yet.

I am learning that fullness of joy and fullness of grace happen when I seek God's presence more than just seeking His helping hand. Joy comes from speaking life. Speaking life leads to joy. This is a cycle that is worth putting on repeat.

I wonder if you believe that joy is part of God's plan for you too.

Here is what I've learned about that:

Here's the deal: God never wanted me to be doing my life on my own power, yet He was not going to push His way into my life of homeschooling and family. Being a loving, patient, gracious God, He was willing to wait for me to say, "God, I need your presence." #Courage #Authenticity #JourneyToJoy

Poems/verses that remind me of God's truth:

A Dance, ordered and graceful, and yet giving an impression of complete and utter freedom, of ineffable joy. As the dance progressed, the movement accelerated, and the pattern became clearer, closer, wind and fire moving together, and there was joy, and song, melody soaring, gathering together as wind and fire united: the birth of a star. (Madeleine L'Engle, *A Wind in the Door*)

Ineffable Joy

I am claiming Ineffable Joy as I gain Freedom.
My Dance is Lighter and becoming more
Graceful and Effortless
as I practice on my Accelerated path—
I am gaining clarity as I experience
the strain between
Wind and Fire, Resilient and Fragile,
Resolute and Cowardly.

TRANSITIONS

Testing my
Resilience and
Allowing God to
Navigate and
Settle my
Insecurities.
Trusting God's
Interventions—
Owning and Letting Go of my
Need for Control:
Surrender

Give thanks in all circumstances, for this is God's will for you in Christ Jesus. (1 Thessalonians 5:18 NIV)

Reflections through music and journaling:

For King & Country's song "joy" has a great reminder to hold on to.

What did you gain from the lyrics of this song?

What is something beautiful that God is doing in your life right now?

What do these definitions mean to you?

Enrapture: Give intense pleasure or joy.
Diffuse: Spread or cause to spread over a wide area or among large number of people: not concentrated.

Closing prayer:

Lord, thank You for Your presence and for the way You speak life
to me. My desire is to speak life to those around me. I want to give
thanks in all circumstances, for I know that this is Your will for me.
(See 1 Thessalonians 5:18.)

Give thanks in all circumstances. (See 1 Thessalonians 5:18.)

K IS FOR

KNOWN

Every part of Scripture is God-breathed and useful one
way or another—showing us truth, exposing our rebel-
lion, correction our mistakes, training us to live God's
way. Through the Word we are put together and shaped up
for the tasks God has for us.
2 Timothy 3:16-17 MSG

KAUAI WAS ONCE AGAIN A time to be close to God. This time
He filled me with a new dream. I will never forget one night; I
couldn't sleep. God spoke to me in the middle of the night:

"Dana, you're pregnant!"
With the laughter of Sarai, I responded with, "Yeah, right!?"
(Note that this is now six years after the shock of our surprise
pregnancy number five.)
"No, really. You are 'expectant with anticipation.' I know you
have a dream to write your story, and I believe you will do this by
the year 2020," was what I heard God telling me in my dream that
night.

This vision to write my story got shelved for a few years as I
focused on getting our two older girls through high school.

Once our older daughters went off to college and the other three children were back in school, I had a bit of an identity crisis. For the first time in eighteen years of parenting, I now had regular pockets of time during the school day to do whatever I wanted.

Here is what I've learned about that:

When I am willing, I can show up and get curious with those around me and be vulnerable and remember that "God sees me through the lens of what Jesus did on the cross. He sees me as my truest, most authentic self. He always sees the bigger picture. He is my best friend, my best advocate, and my safest place as I work on inner transformation" (Marilyn Vancil, *Self to Lose, Self to Find*). This is what I mean to be "known" in my relationships.

I wanted to be seen and known in an intimate way. I have heard intimacy described as "into me see." Unfortunately, I unknowingly create hinderances to this kind of intimacy in all my relationships when I do any of these things:

- worry about or fear being embarrassed
- stay too busy
- become complacent
- fail to prioritize
- lack faith

Poems/verses that remind me of God's truth:

I don't even know myself these days. When I am stuck in unhealthy patterns, I see my life as a wall hanging made of colorful yarn in a blurry arrangement of random stitches. It reminds me of a chaotic scene of a kaleidoscope. I want to see my life as a beautiful, life-sized tapestry. I want to recognize the subtle nuances and marvel at its profound beauty.

This was my heart's cry for quite a while. I may not always be honest about how I feel; however, God always knows. One day I found this verse during my quiet time: "The spirit of man is the lamp of the Lord searching all [their] innermost parts" (Proverbs 20:27 ESV). I heard God speaking directly to me, and I felt seen and known in an intimate way. This is how I heard the verse as it applied to me:

> *Dear one, your spirit, the one that gives you gut reactions and feelings, is Me, is My lamp shedding light on something that you have the power to affect—with the help of My strength in you.*

Reflections through music and journaling:

I hope you find the encouragement needed to let down your walls. You are uniquely put together. I also hope you feel known like I did by listening to the lyrics from "Choose to Love" by Francesca Battestelli.

What did you gain from the lyrics of this song?

Have you let the busyness of life be a wall so no one could get too close?

How do you unknowingly create hinderances to this kind of intimacy in your relationships?

Closing prayer:

Lord, thank You for giving me a mind and a conscience, that I cannot hide from myself. Thank You that Your divine power has given me everything I need for living a godly life, through knowing you. (See Proverbs 20:27 and 2 Peter 1:3–4.)

God sees us as our sees me as my truest, most authentic self.
—Marilyn Vancil

$\mathcal{L}$ IS FOR
LAUGHTER

A cheerful disposition is good for your health;
gloom and doom leave you bone-tired.
Proverbs 17:22 MSG

YOU KNOW HOW IT IS when people ask those awkward questions? When we were expecting our third child after having had two girls, people asked, "So are you hoping for a boy?" as if that was the only conceivable reason to have three children. I smiled and said we'd be happy with either one. Each child is such a gift.

When we were expecting our fourth child, people asked, "So you want a big family?" as if we were crazy. I smiled and said we felt blessed.

When we were expecting our fifth child, people no longer asked questions. They just commented. "Wow!" Once again, I'd smile (and laugh to myself).

It is funny to remember these questions from random people—I didn't care what they thought. However, there were many times when I truly struggled to let go of societal pressures to fit in. I was a complete mess. Tears were a daily issue in our home; either my tears or tears caused by my careless words and actions. There is a song to remind me that we're all broken in some way and we all try to hide what isn't "perfect," but when we "Let the Light In," we can let go of mistakes and learn to laugh ("Let the Light In" by Francesca Battestelli).

I wonder, do you also need to start believing that laughter is part of God's plan for you?

Here's what I've learned about that:

There wasn't much laughter in my life during this season. My dear husband remembered a time many years ago when we went to a show called *Triple Espresso*, on tour in Seattle. I had laughed so hard. Recently, "Mr. Wonderful" planned a surprise trip to Minnesota for us to see this show again. That experience reopened the flow of laughter in me. From this experience, I have learned there is nothing I can do to deserve love like this. I cannot earn it; it is freely given by God *through* my dear husband and other people in my life. My job is to learn how to receive it. I wrote this poem as a reminder that laughter is good medicine.

Poems/verses that remind me of God's truths:

Enjoy Life

The Dance goes on and on;
I hurt therefore I want!
I fear therefore I react!
Then,
You hurt and you want!
You fear and you react!
This dance comes to steal, rob, and destroy!
Stop the Music; change the song.
Stop the tears.
Forgive yourself.
God loves You.
God Delights in You.
Learn to Laugh!

God gave You life to *enjoy*!
Laugh. Play. Sing. Dance.
Learn a different dance.

Rejoice in the Lord always, again I say rejoice. (Philippians 4:4 NKJV)

Let us come before him with thanksgiving and enthusiastically praise him with music and song. (See Psalm 95:2.)

Reflections through music and journaling:

By listening to "Better When I'm Dancin'" by Meghan Trainor, I am learning a new dance.

After you dance to this song, journal what it felt like.

How does this message resonate with you?

What might your tears be telling you?

Are there times when you struggle to let go of societal pressures to fit in? What are they? Why does it matter so much to you to "fit in"?

Closing prayer:

Thank You for creating us to be able to laugh. Thank You for my wonderful husband and special people in my life who love me enough to keep me laughing.

Rejoice in the Lord always. —Philippians 4:4

 IS FOR

MODIFICATIONS

*These words I speak to you are not incidental additions
to your life, homeowner improvements to your standard of
living. They are foundational words to build a life on. If
you work these words into your life, you are like a smart
carpenter who built his house on solid rock. Rain poured
down, the river flooded, a tornado hit—but nothing
moved the house. It was fixed on the rock.*
Matthew 7:24–25 MSG

MY HUSBAND AND I HAVE done many remodeling projects together over the past twenty-nine years of marriage. He is an amazing visionary. He can move walls in his mind and tell me how it will be, but I cannot fully conceptualize the final look. I have learned to trust him because we do great work together, and the end result always exceeds my vision.

While remodeling a house, I have seen this evolution:

- Demolition: clearing out all that is not working well, with a vision for what it could look like.
- Redesign: changing walls around for better function.
- Rebuilding: sometimes the longest stage.
- Finish work: the trim and details.
- Decorating: making decisions together for mutual enjoyment.

I have a parallel for these five stages in my marriage and in my life in Christ. At times, my husband and I have built our home and our marriage in haphazard ways, not always seeking God's help. Sometimes we need to go through a demolition process to tear down the relational walls we've built up. After such a time, my husband and I need God to help us with visualizing what changes to make. Then, we will need tools and helpers for the rebuilding. This phase often has times of fast progress intermixed with times of slower, less visible progress. The finish work and decorating stages can be fun and energizing and mutually satisfying, but also expensive. But here's the good news: emotional love can be rebuilt.

When God looks at us, he doesn't see what's wrong. He only sees what's missing. He is rubbing his hands together, as if to say, "Hey, let's do something amazing with this part of your life!"

If we are willing to go through this messy process, God can do more than remodel us—He can work wonders in our relationships.

What might happen if you started believing that modifications are part of God's plan for you?

Here's what I've learned about that:

Back in F is for Favor, I mentioned how I borrowed my first life verse from Graham Cooke. Let me reiterate it here for easier reference:

> Fear not [there is nothing to fear], for I am with you: do not look around you in terror and be dismayed, for I am your God. I will strengthen you and harden you to difficulties, yes, I will help you; yes, I will hold you up and retain you with my [victorious] right hand of rightness and justice. For I the Lord your God hold your right hand; I am the Lord, Who says to you, Fear not; I will help you! Fear not, you worm of Jacob, you (people) of Israel! I will help you, says the Lord; your Redeemer is the Holy One of Israel. Behold, I will make you to

be a new, sharp, threshing instrument, which has teeth; you shall thresh the mountains and beat them small, and shall make the hills like chaff. (Isaiah 41:11, 13–15 amp, author emphasis)

Okay, wow! God had some powerful lessons in here for me.

God continues to make modifications in my heart. I am becoming a *threshing instrument* with teeth to chew up mountains of grief, of challenge, of disappointment, to make them small, like chaff; to separate the grain from the stalk. I continue the process of *thrashing/threshing* myself from my family of origin/the plant. I am learning to separate out issues and ideas to see what is mine to own and let the rest fall away with the wind. God is *sharpening* me to do the work needed to separate from my disappointments and resentments in my relationships.

God is giving me grit and a voice to be strong and courageous and to tear into mountains of hurt so that they become small. I heard the Holy Spirit's voice. (See more in "R Is for Resilience.")

Poems/verses that remind me of God's truth:

Now we look inside, and what we see is that anyone united with the Messiah gets a fresh start. (2 Corinthians 5:17 msg)

Now God has us where he wants us, with all the time in this world and the next to shower grace and kindness upon us in Christ Jesus. Saving is all his idea, and all his work. All we do is trust him enough to let him do it. It's God's gift from start to finish! We don't play the major role. If we did, we'd probably go around bragging that we'd done the whole thing! No, we neither make nor save ourselves. God does both the making and saving. He creates each of us by Christ Jesus to join him in the work he does, the good work he has gotten ready for us to do, work we had better be doing. (Ephesians 2:7–10 MSG)

Reflections through music and journaling:

The song "Better Together" by JJ Heller is a reminder to me that my priority is to make modifications and mature in my love and partnership with my husband.

What stage in the remodeling process are you in right now?

How does this page help you process through that stage?

What are your next steps?

Closing prayer:

Lord, thank You for Your great grace that allows us to make modifications and to start over at any point in our lives. Thank You for Your guiding principles in the Bible.

_____

_____

_____

_____

_____

_____

_____

_____

_____

The good news is, emotional love can be rebuilt.

 IS FOR

NEEDS

So we're not giving up. How could we! Even though on the
outside it often looks like things are falling apart on us, on
the inside, where God is making new life, not a day goes
by without his unfolding grace.
2 Corinthians 4:17 MSG

WHEN OUR KIDS WERE SIX, four, and two, I just had to have a dog. My life was pretty full with a kindergartner, a preschooler, a two-year-old, and now . . . a puppy. What was I thinking?

Then, hello. I was pregnant . . . again. My immediate panicked thought was, *We need to move. Our house is too small for a family of six!* My husband and I got busy and finished all the projects around the house in order to sell it. I guess you could call it a major case of nesting.

On moving day, our oldest turned seven and I was now six months pregnant and on bed rest. As we moved to our new home just one mile away, I began my training in admitting I had needs and learning how to ask for and receive help. God was giving me a chance to start over, to set up a new home with new routines. I could stop wandering around in the wilderness of worry and start letting go of control and receiving God's love *through* other people rather being the doer and giver I had prided myself in.

As I let other people pick up my kids from school, playdates, and activities as well as unpack and arrange my whole house, and, oh right, walk the dog, I grew in my recognition of how much God cared for me.

Here's what I've learned about that:

It took me a long time to realize that I wasn't a failure for having needs. I just had needs. My encouragement to you is to let your needs be known: It's okay—you're not a failure. You don't always have to be the one giving and doing. You can ask for patience and kindness from those around you. It may take embracing the realities of vulnerability, but, trust me, it will be worth it, as it leads to new life. #Courage #Authenticity #BecomingMyBestPossibleSelf

Poems/verses that remind me of God's truth:

VULNERABILITY

Visible and invisible:
Undeniably in need of
Loving support;
Needing
Effort to
Restore my trust in other's
Affection:
Boldness
In
Love; Living
In
Truth to restore
Your relationships.

NEEDS are . . .

Nonjudgmental, **E**nigmatic, **E**quivocal, **D**ependable and **S**ubject to . . .
so many variables.

God's mercies are new every morning. (See Lamentations 3:23)

Reflections through music and journaling:

Francesca Battestelli has a playful reminder in her song "This Is The Stuff." We all have different needs every day, but God is always with us.

Are you able to let your needs be known, or has bitterness seeped into your life?

Can you give it to God to transform?

Where do you need refreshment right now?

Can you just ask for a day off? Why or why not? What would you do with a day off?

Closing prayer:

Thank You, Lord, for the way You use everything in my daily life to show me that You care enough to meet my needs.

God is always there with me; he gives me new life.

O IS FOR

OBEDIENCE

*Give your entire attention to what God is doing right
now, and don't get worked up about what may or may not
happen tomorrow.*
Matthew 6:34 MSG

MY FAVORITE PAINTING IS ONE painted by my mother-in-law
of a road that bends so you cannot see around the corner (see cover
picture). This has become a metaphor I use in discerning what obedience looks like during life's decisions and disruptions.

Each spring we would assess the progress of each child and
discern if homeschooling was working for them. Since every child
is different, we didn't want to make a broad choice to homeschool
everyone every year. There came a time when our son needed more
activity and interactions than we could provide with a house full
of sisters, so we found a traditional school setting for him. That
worked for a year or two, and then it was time to reevaluate again.

At each crossroad I didn't know what next week or next year
would look like, but *I knew that I knew that I knew* that I needed
to take the next obedient step and trust that a future step would be
revealed at the right moment. I think this is what Emily P. Freeman
is talking about in *The Next Right Thing*.

Obedience brings security and confidence: that clear, peaceful feeling of knowing you are where you are supposed to be and do-ing what you are supposed to do. I have heard it said that delayed action is disobedience. When faced with a challenge, I want my first response to be one of obedience and optimism and to trust the outcome to God's capable hands.

I have noticed that distraction and disruptions can be an ene-my to my desire to listen and obey verses like, "Stay with God! Take heart. Don't quit!" (Psalm 27:14 MSG).

Here's what I've learned about that:

When frustration with schoolwork and an inability to commu-nicate effectively with teachers led us to try a different school for one year, and when that year turned into another year and another school, I knew it was time for help. My son's self-esteem had plum-meted.

I can't remember how we first heard of Lehman Learning Solu-tions, but it was truly an answer to our heart-wrenching prayers for our child. School/academic work was not life giving for this child. This child's brain was wired in such a way that made the job of being a student difficult. Thanks to Cindy Lehman and the wonderful specialists, we were given a new hope that our child's brain could be rewired to do what it was being asked to do. Our child didn't need drugs to help him focus and stay on task. Our child thought he was the only one who couldn't do the work and was questioning their worthiness. With therapeutic brain exercises, LLS helped my child's self-esteem take a 180-degree turn.

This season was full of disruptions in the life of our family. I worked diligently to practice obedience in light of these disruption. During this time, I was reminded of when I had read *Rising Strong* by Brené Brown.

Poems/verses that remind me of God's truth:

Brené Brown challenged me to believe that disruptions can actually be helpful in my journey when I reframe them.

DISRUPTIONS

Disturbances that
Interrupt my
Sacred Rituals;
Redirecting me to
Use caution and to
Pause: Leading me to
Transitions:
Initiating change;
Other directions I could go.
Needing to learn to let go.
Surrender.

RISING STRONG

Rumble with and get Curious:
Inquire about my own
Story. Letting
Intuition
Nurture my heart: Being
Generous with myself and others.

Scoffers will
Test my
Resilience:
Opening up my
New Story: The one I can write the ending for.
Growth!

I am not abandoned. The Father is with me. I've told you all this so that trusting me, you will be unshakable and assured, deeply at peace. (John 16:33 MSG)

Reflections through music and journaling:

My feeling of *I know that I know that I know* gives me the courage to take a leap of faith like Matthew West sings about in "All In."

Try writing your own acrostic poem about some of your distractions.

What is something you need guidance and direction for right now?

My hope for you is to be brave enough to be obedient.

What would obedience look like in your situation?

Closing prayer:

Lord, when I am faced with disruptions, I want my response to be one of obedience and optimism as I trust the outcome into Your capable hands.

_____

_____

_____

_____

_____

_____

_____

_____

_____

Stay with God! Take heart. Don't quit! —Psalm 27:14 MSG

P IS FOR

PRIORITIES

*I know what I am doing. I have it all planned out - plans
to take care of you, not abandon you.*
Jeremiah 29:11 MSG

OUR CHOSEN LIFESTYLE OF HOMESCHOOLING our kids provided lots of togetherness. This was wonderful as well as draining. There came a time and a need for the kids to be involved in activities outside the home. With multiple children in multiple activities, life could quickly get complicated and overscheduled. We worked diligently to keep a balance, allowing one activity to each of the older three children for one season, then a season of doing one activity together.

While reflecting together on our separate childhoods, my husband and I realized neither of us had close friendships that continued from that time. We decided to be the main constant in our children's growing repertoire of relationships. We prioritized going to each of their sporting events and theater performances as a family. We also prioritized family vacations: road trips and sailing trips. These extended vacations planted rich memories of togetherness.

When we reached the high school years of our homeschool journey, there was constant chatter in our co-op community among the moms. It was easy to fall into the traps of comparison about test scores, transcripts, and college applications. I was gently reminded of Jeremiah 29:11.

This verse was one of the verses chosen for our oldest daughter for her baptism. God's gentle spirit reminded me that this verse was applicable to me as well. I felt challenged to admit that I believe this verse to be true. I thanked God that he had my daughter's life planned out and that I needn't feel abandoned during this college-prep season. I prayed for the Lord to help me slow down and seek and trust His leading. He has always had every detail of my life and my children's lives in his capable hands. I needed to keep looking to him for guidance and direction.

As I mentioned in "B Is for Belonging," I don't regret the intentional choices we made in our family. Our intentionality has given our children a strong sense of knowing where they belong.

I challenge you to wonder if prioritizing God might be part of His plan for you.

Here's what I've learned about that:

We lost my mom when baby Grace was five months old. My mom left us a rich legacy of love. I was so grateful for our homeschool journey that enabled us to create these lasting memories with my mom while we could.

In "C Is for Connection," I talked about the year of life and death while my mom battled ALS. We learned so much about life that year. During our special visits, we learned what it meant to practice presence. We are all so grateful for setting that priority. #NoRegrets

As I continue to grow, I strive to practice living in the present moment and being aware of my strengths as well as my blind spots. I am routinely reminded how vitally important it is to be patient with myself, my husband, and my kids. #Authenticity #Integrity #StayAwayFromEasy

Poems/verses that remind me of God's truth:

Dear Lord Jesus,

Help me slow down. It always goes better with you leading. I need Your wisdom and Your guidance. I need patience to wait for Your leading, and the courage to obey and prioritize your nudges . . . today and every day.

In need of your support,
Your Dear One

Dear One,

Rather than planning and evaluating, practice trusting and thanking Me continually. Learn to take time to play instead of constant productivity and exhaustion. Keep looking to Me for guidance and direction.

With all my love and devotion,
Your Lord Jesus

> The Lord is my comfort. I lack nothing. He leads me to quiet waters and refreshes my soul. (See Psalm 23:1–3.)

> Be still and know that I am God. (Psalm 46:10 NIV)

Reflections through music and journaling:

As I practice listening to words like the prayer above, I want my priority to be a heart full of words, like Lauren Daigle sings about in "I Am Yours."

Are you willing to let the Holy Spirit help you set priorities that align with God's will?

What would that require of you?

Do you believe that you are God's number one priority?

What would it take to believe?

Closing prayer:

Lord, thank You for Your promises that remind me that You have all my life planned out. I pray for a stronger sense of being able to believe that "I am Yours."

Let the peace of Christ rule in your heart.
Colossians 3:15 NIV

 IS FOR

QUIET

I have told you these things so that in Me you may have
perfect peace. In the world you have tribulation and
distress and suffering, but be courageous, be confident, be
undaunted, be filled with joy; I have overcome the world.
My conquest is accomplished; My victory abiding.
John 16:33 AMP

THERE WAS A TIME WHEN my son was in middle school and was struggling to put forth what I thought was adequate effort in his schoolwork. During this time, God was teaching me to keep my comments to myself, to be quiet. We had recently returned from a Mexico mission trip, where my son had made a special connection to one of the orphans, Sergio. My son was impacted by the reality that despite his desire, Sergio was not allowed to go to school.

One day when I was frustrated that my son was choosing not to put finishing detail on his work, I wondered if he'd forgotten about Sergio already and taken for granted his own learning opportunity. Thankfully, I kept my mouth quiet.

Later that day, my son shared an interaction he'd had at school. My son was able to share his experience from Mexico and challenge a fellow student to take his learning more seriously. I realized my son gets it. He doesn't always act like it, but he gets it. I needed the reminder that if I truly trust that God has a plan for my son's life, I can be quiet.

Through the storms of my life, I have experienced regret and frustration. I shared earlier that there was a time when I felt no peace and no joy. I have come to know peace and know joy through the exercise of stillness. I am better able to hear God's voice and be inspired to continue on my journey of lifelong learning if I take time to be quiet in God's presence. If I breathe slowly and deeply, if I relax in His holy presence while His face shines upon me, I can receive His peace. Be quiet: enjoy peace.

I challenge you to consider that listening to God might be part of His plan for you. Quit striving and be quiet.

Here's what I've learned about that:

Through the exercise of stillness, I am able to hear God's voice more clearly. This clarity affects all of the areas of life on my adventure of lifelong learning.

It is in my still moments that I feel inspired to write poems and prayers.

Poems/verses that remind me of God's truth:

Be still and know that I am God. (Psalm 46:10 NIV)

STILLNESS

Silent
Thoughts.
Inspiration.
Listening and
Learning.
Nothing
Else!
Sit
Still!

The Lord make his face shine upon you and be gracious to you; the Lord turn his face toward you and give you peace. (Numbers 6:25–26 NIV)

QUIET

Quit
Underestimating me:
I can be
Eternally
Trusted

Are you tired? Worn out? Burned out on religion? Come to me. Get away with me and you'll recover your life. I'll show you how to take a real rest. Walk with me and work with me—watch how I do it. Learn the unforced rhythms of grace. I won't lay anything heavy or ill-fitting on you. Keep company with me and you'll learn to live freely and lightly. (Matthew 11:28–30 MSG)

REST

Reflect.
Expect.
Seek and
Trust.

Reflections through music and journaling:

When I am quiet and quit striving, I am in the best position to embrace the words of Casting Crowns' song "Just Be Held."
Respond to the music.
Respond to these quotes:

Peace and love are alive in us, but we are not always alive in peace and love. —Julian of Norwich

Gratitude, in itself, is heaven. Gratitude is heaven itself; there could be no heaven without gratitude. (William Blake)

What are you grateful for?

Where can you find quiet today?

Rewrite Psalm 23 in your own words. What does it say about being quiet?

Closing prayer:

Lord, thank You for all the reminders of what You want to pour into me, when I take the time to be quiet.

Gratitude is heaven itself. —William Blake

$\mathcal{R}$ IS FOR
RESILIENCE

He energizes those who get tired, gives fresh strength to
dropouts. For even young people tire and drop out. . . .
But those who wait upon God get fresh strength.
Isaiah 40:30 MSG

IN THE PAST I HAD strong needs and innate desires for peace and oneness, and I needed to feel comfortable and settled. I was afraid of conflict and feeling invisible or insignificant. I was hesitant to be brave and step out in love and self-respect to share my desire to be seen and to feel relevant. I craved compassion and consideration, so it was scary to end up in a place of misunderstanding or uncertainty of my worth of someone's consideration.

To me there is an element of wisdom and discernment needed for resilience. James 1:5 is a solid reminder that wisdom is freely given to all who ask for it. My lessons in resilience came through my yearlong study of the enneagram (an ancient typology tool for understanding personalities) that led me to believe I was what is described as a withdrawing type.

When I sought the wisdom and discernment promised to me in James, I was able to see more clearly what was happening in my interactions with people in my life who were assertive. As I changed my approach in my interactions, I saw that my people were confused and unnerved by my new approach. As I practiced using my voice more than withdrawing, sometimes it caused stress and unpleasant feelings to those I was interacting with. I still need to practice my new technique—however with wisdom, I now have tools to progress through my resilience training and stay away from feeling attacked.

I was reminded of my starter verse from Graham Cooke. The Holy Spirit gently said,

Dana, I am transforming you from "insignificant" and "defensive" to an instrument with strong, sharp teeth to remove unwanted life-choking elements so that your mountains of misery and envy will be smooth and your 'tough old hills' [a.k.a. my hardened heart] will become rich fertile ground to rebuild upon."

#Resilience

Here's what I've learned about that:

I continue to work at staying away from defensiveness. Instead of indulging in feelings of regret that eventually lead to resentment, I want to accept my shortcomings so that I can know peace. I am practicing recognizing that when things don't go as planned, I can be sure God never leaves me. He is always there with me, even when I have doubts and regrets. Resilience is learning to run freely and living in a new understanding of how God sees me! For me, when I am honest with my people, it helps everyone be able to bounce back with resilience.

I have needed to use the following words more times than I'd like to admit.

Dear Loved One of Mine,

I am recognizing the hurt in your heart. I am recognizing the pain of my hurtful words. I see the pain in your eyes. I see the pain in your posture. I have wounded you with careless, disrespectful words and disrespectful actions. I cannot take them back, and I cannot undo the hurt. The scars may last forever. I ask that you would forgive me. I want to begin to rebuild a relationship that is mutually respectful and mutually satisfying. I love you. I desire for you to be free from the anger and resentment going on between us.

Love, Me

Poems/verses that remind me of God's truth:

REJOICE!

Remember
Everyday
Journeys.
Open up to what
I (God)
Can do for you
Enjoy life!

RESILIENCE

Raise questions and get Curious about
Equanimity. How does it affect my
Story. Let
Intuition
Lighten my heart: Be
Inquisitive and
Engage with
New ideas.
Challenge myself to
Embrace Rejoicing!

Look to the Lord and His strength; seek His face always. (Psalm 105:4 NIV)

Reflections through music and journaling:

> Resilience is remembering and rejoicing in promises, like Chris Tomlin sings about in "Amazing Grace (My Chains Are Gone)."

> Do you believe that we can rejoice in these promises? Tell God about your regrets and get ready to move on. What is next for you?

Closing prayer:

Lord, thank You for the wisdom available to me when I ask. Thank You for caring enough for me to release the chains that bind me. Thank You for Your amazing grace.

_____

_____

_____

_____

_____

_____

_____

_____

_____

_____

Courage doesn't mean we're not afraid anymore, it just means our
lives aren't controlled by our doubts. —Bob Goff

S IS FOR
SELF-CONTROL

Delight yourself in the Lord and he will give you the
desires of your heart. Commit your way to the Lord; trust
in him and he will do this: He will make your righteous
reward shine like the dawn, the justice of your cause like
the noonday sun.
(Psalm 37:4-6, author's paraphrase)

ONE DAY DURING MY QUIET time, I found the verse above. It felt like a direct message from God. I rewrote the verse in the way I heard the word from God and wrote this prayer as a response.

Keep company with God; get in on the best. Find great pleasure and satisfaction in spending [quiet] time with the Lord. He will give you what you crave and the secret longings of your heart (Psalm 37:4–6, author's paraphrase)

Lord,

I am laying it all out for you, my secret cravings to have better self-control. I ask that you would blaze a trail before me that will lead to joy.

Set me at the right pace for each stretch of the journey—fast, steady, slow jog, walk . . . When you see me crawling, I trust that your hand will pick me up so I can keep going.

I mentioned in D is for Dream that another secret longing I had was to write a book. As I continued to read books that stretched me, I continued to journal. As my journals became full of reflections, prayers, and poems as a response to this growth, I realized I *was* writing my book!

However, I was still afraid to move forward with my vision to actually write a book, until I read James 1:25 (MSG): "Whoever catches a glimpse of the revealed counsel of God—the free life!-- even out of the corner of (their) eye, and sticks with it, is no distracted scatterbrain but a (person) of action. That person will find delight and affirmation in the action."

Receiving this encouraging and validating God hug, I decided to *go for it*! For me to recognize and embrace the godly design of self-control and move forward in writing my book, I needed my previous lessons in reliance training and being quiet with God.

Here's what I've learned about that:

One of my favorite memories in Hawaii was when my family went to Chief Sielu Avea's plantation. I picked my first guava off of a tree and ate it. It was delicious. After that, I researched guava. I learned it was considered a super fruit. That got me thinking of the fruit of the Spirit. I wrote this poem about the super fruit of self-control.

Poems/verses that remind me of God's truth:

I am the Lord your God who will take hold of your hand. Do not fear: I will help you. (See Isaiah 41:13)

Whether you turn to the right or to the left, your ears will hear a voice behind you, saying, "This is the way; walk in it." (Isaiah 30:21 NIV)

SELF-CONTROL

Self-control is that fruit that no one notices if
you are doing it well—
but everyone notices when you miss the mark.
It's that fruit that packs a bonus blessing—
Humility.
We all want it.
We all need it—
that pleasure of knowing that we are in sync with
God's will;
when we hold our tongue or
harness our thoughts.
But would it be appropriate to tell others, "Hey,
if you only knew what I wanted to say right now,
but had the self-control not to, you'd be so proud
of me."
Humility.
Self-control.
Hard to come by:
Delicious and worth the wait.
Leaves you craving more.

SURRENDER

Strength in yielding.
Undoing
Resistance;
Relenting;
Enduring shame from others.
No longer needing to
Defend my motives.
Enemies silenced;
Respect reciprocated.

Reflections through music and journaling:

Practicing self-control is like surrendering to God's authority. Lauren Daigle sings about this in "You Have My Surrender."

Write a response to the message of James 1:2 (MSG):

> Consider it a sheer gift, friends, when tests and challenges come at you from all sides. You know that under pressure, your faith-life is forced into the open and shows its true colors.

What are your secret longings?

How do the words of this song encourage you in the areas of surrender and secret longings?

Write out the fruit of the Spirit in your journal and write one or two ways you can be mindful of them today and through the week ahead. (See Galatians 5:22–23.)

Closing prayer:

Lord, I thank You for the lessons You have given me to learn and practice self-control. The reward has been a warm reassurance "like the noonday sun." (See Psalm 37:4–6.)

The fruit of the Spirit is Love, Joy, Peace, Patience, Kindness, Gentleness, and Self-Control. (See Galatians 5:22–23.)

T IS FOR

TRUTH

You are truly my disciples if you remain faithful to my teachings. And you will know the truth, and the truth will set you free.
John 8:31–32 NIV

I HAVE A CONFESSION. FOR YEARS I had been parenting on my own strength. The Lord stirred my heart and revealed that I had become critical and resentful. I was trying to motivate my kids with a frown on my face. God's Spirit wanted to help me, but there was a kink in the flow. God is a patient parent Who won't push His way into my life. Once I asked for help, I was able to gradually receive it and go to my kids, gather them up, and cherish them, contributing to peace and healing in our home.

When we decided to take our kids out of school and try homeschooling to regroup, rekindle, and renew as a family, I was so excited to start the adventure. We agreed to take one year off from the chaos of overscheduling and then reevaluate. I was hopeful and energized and also fully aware of my need for God's help.

One of my favorite songs growing up was "The Warrior Is a Child" by Twila Paris. I sang it in front of my church in eighth grade. Recently I was reminded of a line of lyric that implies that people see me as strong and capable, yet the truth is I run to my heavenly Father and ask for His strong hands to protect me. I wonder if this is true for you too. I wonder why I hide my true feelings. I want to get real and start being more truthful about my feelings and my struggles.

I challenge you to start believing that speaking truth and living in truth is part of God's plan for you as well.

Here's what I've learned about that:

Everyone knows it's better to be honest, but it isn't easily done. In fact, there are many song lyrics reminding us. "If We're Honest" by Francesca Battestelli reveals that when we're honest, healing for our brokenness is available.

For many of the years of raising my family and homeschooling, I was not honest with my needs. I needed help but didn't know how to ask for it. I have learned that living in truth and honesty takes tenacity—firm obstinance or continuance in a course of action in spite of difficulty or opposition.

Poems/verses that remind me of God's truth:

I want to choose **Truth and Grace**—

Trusting in the
Restorative
Uplifting
Tenderness of my
Heavenly parent
and
Gently
Reaching out
And
Choosing courage:
Ending the silence.

Stay with God! Take heart. Don't quit. I'll say it again: Stay with God. (Psalm 27:14 MSG)

Surely God is my salvation: I will trust and not be afraid. The Lord is my strength and my song; He has become my salvation. (Isaiah 12:2-3 NIV)

Nothing is impossible with God! (Luke 1:37 NIV)

Reflections through music and journaling:

If we know that it's better to tell the truth, why is it so hard to be honest? I think it's because of fear. Let's practice the tough-minded energy of not being afraid and staying away from the lies that Matthew West sings about in "Truth Be Told." This approach releases the flow of redemptive energy available to us through the Holy Spirit.

What are you afraid of?

Do you believe the promise above in Luke 1:37?

Write yourself a letter of encouragement.

Closing prayer:

Thank you, Lord, that there are so many reminders of the benefits of telling the truth, seeking truth, and living a life of truth.

Nothing is impossible with God!

U IS FOR

UNBOUNDED

The Lord is my strength and my shield; my heart trusts in him, and I am helped. My heart leaps for joy and I will give thanks to him in song.
Psalm 28:7 NIV

WHEN I ENCOUNTER UNEXPECTED CHANGES, I don't always have an adequate supply of flexibility and grace. These are times when I feel limited, finite, inadequate. My need for God's unbounded presence in my life requires self-awareness. For me to upgrade my identity is to learn about Who God is: unchanging, unfailing, relentless. But here's the deal: self-awareness, self-knowledge, and self-acceptance all mean looking at my weaknesses as well as my strengths. It requires an act of bravery for me to live into this kind of identity for myself. I am slowly learning how to upgrade my identity and claim unbounded strength from God!

I want to have the character that Francesca Battestelli sings about in "Unusual." As I learn more about myself through the lens of the enneagram, I recognize that I am not afraid to be strange or unique. So, to build my character, I am learning to recognize that it's important to connect and communicate clearly in all my relationships. It could be as simple as letting people know that I heard them and understand where they are coming from, even if I do not agree with them. I needn't take their words as criticism or intended conflict.

However, this also requires me to recognize that good communication is a delicate dance of what I say and how I say it. One of the new dance steps that is still tricky for me is how I let others know I respect their opinion and care enough to stay in conversation with them rather than withdrawing or trying to change them. All of these areas that I am trying to improve require me to access the unbounded love of my heavenly Parent.

I challenge you to start believing the unbounded Source of life you have as a favored child of God.

What I have learned about that:

Once again, the Bible offers examples of God's unbounded love for us.

> The righteous give and give; generous gets it all in the end. Stalwart walks in step with God; their step is blazed by God and is happy. If I stumble, I won't be down for long; God has a grip on my hand and will pick me up. (See Psalm 37:21–23.)

Having the ability to live into this verse requires an act of unbounded bravery.

Poems/verses that remind me of God's truth:

> If God is for us, who can be against us? (Romans 8:31 NIV)

BRAVERY

Believe Truth!
Remember to move on.
Accept Joyfully. Gain
Victory over
Enemies.
Redirect thoughts, say
Yes to deeper understanding!

On the Wings of Eagles

Endings and beginnings anew
Are opportunities to stretch and grow;
Failures are a possibility for a new chance.
I will decide to fight with a lance
To ward off evil's demise
And seek God's favor and to rise
Above the ashes of doubt and fear;
My time of peace and joy are near;
Goals are for those who are strong,
The journey may seem endlessly long;
When people challenge me to prove even,
I must remember my reward is in heaven;
I want to fight the good fight,
To soar on wings in Jesus's light.

Reflections through music and journaling:

The song "Unusual" by Francesca Battestelli reminds us that it is not our job to fit in. We are called to a higher identity, and we are able to answer that call by claiming God's unbounded promises to carry us.

How are you feeling limited?

Are you willing to let go and receive God's unbounded strength?

What would feeling brave look like for you? Feel like?

Look up Psalm 37. How might you be transformed by unbounded hope in these promises?

Closing prayer:

Lord, thank You for Your unbounded love. Lead me and guide me to live into my transformed identity with bravery.

The Lord gave us mind and conscience; we cannot hide
from ourselves. —Proverbs 20:27 GNT

V IS FOR

VIRTUE

Search me, oh God, and know my heart;
test me and know my anxious thoughts.
Psalm 139:23 NLT

As I continue to learn about the strengths and weaknesses of my personality type, I am beginning to find my voice and grow in understanding myself better. During stressful times and intense interactions, I have the tendency to wallow in feelings of envy—my vice.

> Envy: a feeling of discontented or resentful longing: a desire to have a quality, possession, or desirable attribute belonging to someone else.

When I can pause and breathe, I can get to a more secure mind space. This allows me to work on looking at the situation with equanimity.

> Equanimity: mental calmness, composure, and evenness of temper, especially in a difficult situation.

I am learning to recognize when my vice starts to show up,

which means I can choose a more virtuous response. My ultimate goal is to stop devaluing myself, to fight against my needs for love and care without sinking into shame, envy, or feeling inferior for having these needs. However, when I take on a withdrawing stance and freeze during conflict, that takes me to a place of extreme vulnerability. Being between these two extremes is where I experience my growing pains. Ancara imparo. Always learning.

I challenge you to wonder if learning to recognize your unhealthy responses and trading them for healthier responses is part of God's plan for you.

What I have learned about that:

As I get real about what it means to have a more virtuous response, I am leaning into being vulnerable and striving for more equanimity.

Poems/verses that remind me of God's truth:

Vice to Virtue

When I feel utterly out of control
Grasping at anything is not wise.
I grope and grab as my only vice—
But into God's merciful arms I must go.
God, come to my rescue and support
My efforts to build a home—
A place where all can come;
A peaceful, supportive fort.
Come fill my heart with kindness:
Each day brings a new test.
Fill my void and give me rest.
Please, I pray—lead me to forgiveness.
Different views of life are real to me and you.

Grace is needed: self-control and wisdom.

Into your arms of empathy and compassion I
come.

Letting go and embracing them is my goal: virtue.

VULNERABLE

Vice to Virtue;
Undeniably in need of
Loving support;
No need for
Envy.
Remembering to
Alter my thoughts.
Believing the Best.
Learning about
Equanimity!

EQUANIMITY

Evenness:
Quit devaluing yourself.
Understand what your
Anxiety is telling you.
Nothing is wrong with you, say
I am enough.
Mental calmness
Is your
Ticket on
Your path to Virtue.

Reflections through music and journaling:

As I practice having a more virtuous response in stressful situations, I want to recall the words of "The Change in Me" by Casting Crowns.

Can you honestly pray this Scripture verse?

> Search me, oh God, and know my heart; test me and know my anxious thoughts. (Psalm 139:23 NLT)

How might you navigate your current challenge if you believed that God knows your heart?

Closing prayer:

Thank You, Lord, for the powerful reminder that you are a gentle God even when I need your transforming work in me to trade my vice for virtue.

_____

_____

_____

_____

_____

_____

_____

_____

_____

_____

_____

_____

_____

_____

_____

_____

_____

_____

Look to the Lord and His strength; seek his face always.
——Psalm 105:4 NIV

 IS FOR

WORRY

Turn your worries into prayers. Before you know it, a
sense of God's wholeness, everything coming together for
good, will come and settle you down. It's wonderful what
happens when Christ displaces worry at the center
of our life.
Philippians 4:6–7 MSG

WORRY—TO ALLOW ONE'S MIND TO dwell on difficulties or
troubles; agonize, lose sleep, get worked up.

There are so many ways that worry and anxiety creep into my
thoughts. I've had seasons that felt so lonely, like I was in a desert
wasteland. The Bible is full of reminders of how unproductive it is
to worry. During my wilderness experiences, I need daily practice
to learn how to wrap my worry into a prayer, to trade my worry
and take a willing stance to journey with God.

"The Wilderness indeed is a place where God takes you [me] so
that He can speak kindly to you [me] and opens up the next part
of your [my] inheritance" (Graham Cooke).

Graham Cooke has challenged me to let go of worry and wonder what God might replace it with.

If I let go of . . .		**I can receive . . .**
misery	————————————	joy
sadness	————————————	forgiveness
blame	————————————	courage
anger	————————————	fullness
control	————————————	wisdom
pride	————————————	intimacy
fear	————————————	power
shame	————————————	boldness
guilt	————————————	blessings
selfishness	————————————	freedom
lies	————————————	mercy
regrets	————————————	grace
baggage	————————————	desires of my heart

Joy, courage, and wisdom are so much better than misery, blame, and control.

I challenge you to start the practice of trading worry for wonder as part of God's plan for you.

What I have learned about that:

When I get stuck in worry, I want to wonder what it would look like to wake up to my personality type. It requires purposefully thinking, feeling, and acting with more self-awareness. It's like following the arrow of integration on the enneagram map. As a four, I tend to move to one in health. This allows me to "actively shift my attention to see the positive" (*Complete Enneagram* by Beatrice Chestnut, p. 295). See diagram below.

Ancara imparo: always learning.

#BecomingTheBestVersionOfMyself

Poems/verses that remind me of God's truth:

WEARY

Weepy
Exhausted
Apprehensive
Restless
Yearning for Rest and Tenderness

WILDERNESS 1

Wide eyed
Intentionality to
Lean into the
Discomfort:
Embracing the
Rumblings of Regret
Not for the faint of Heart!
Exciting.
Surrendering to
Servanthood

WILDERNESS 2

Wonder,
Interdependence,
Learning and
Discerning:
Excited about no more
Rumblings of Regret—
Not for the faint of Heart!
Embracing
Servanthood and
Surrender!

You will find me when you seek me with all your heart. (Jeremiah 29:13 NIV)

Oh, Lord, you have searched me and you know me. You know when I sit down and when I rise up; you discern my thoughts from afar. (Psalm 139:1–2 NIV)

Reflections through music and journaling:

I wonder what would happen if I practiced believing the words that Switchfoot sings about in "I Won't Let You Go"?

What do you need to release control of?

With what might God replace it with in your life?

What might God want to give you today? This week? This year?

Closing prayer:

Lord, thank You that You care enough for me to give me a better solution than to be weighed down from worry.

Joy, Courage, and Wisdom are so much better than misery,
blame, and control.

 IS FOR

XENIA

(HOSPITALITY IN GREEK)

Love your neighbor as yourself.
Matthew 22:39 NIV

HOSPITALITY IS THE FRIENDLY AND generous reception and entertainment of guests, visitors, or strangers.

My husband and I have made a life pursuit of practicing hospitality. In our twenty-nine years of marriage, at least twenty different people have lived with us for extended periods. We believe that as we steward our blessings, we are called to share them to bless others. By opening our home to so many different individuals, we have been stretched to learn what we are like at our best and our worst. We have also learned many lessons about grace, forgiveness, and love.

It isn't just through hosting friends and acquaintances in our home that we are able to practice hospitality. Our pastor once challenged us to look at our children as the most important houseguest we will ever have.

"True hospitality is welcoming the stranger on their own terms. This kind of hospitality can only be offered by those who've found the center of their lives in their own hearts" (Henry Nouwen).

The story of the prodigal son returning home offers an example of the "true hospitality" that Henry Nouwen describes, as the father insisted on throwing a party to his son's liking.

This is also the kind of hospitality we strive for while building houses in Tijuana. We ask the homeowner where they want the doors and windows and what exterior paint color they want so that the house feels like their own home.

I challenge you to start believing that practicing hospitality is part of God's plan for you.

What I have learned about that:

Steven Arterburn admits, "It may be true that a life of isolation is easier, but it's also a lot emptier" (*New Life Daily Devotional*, "The Disconnected Life").

When I am tempted to isolate and withdraw, I want to heed the warning that "[to] grow comfortable [we] stop developing into what God wants." As I write this book, it is becoming clearer to me that I need to practice hospitality to myself as well. Call it self-care, call it kindness or self-love, but I believe xenia is what Jesus was talking about in his commandment to love yourself *as* (in the same way) you love others (Matthew 22:39, emphasis added).

I appreciate Bob Goff's book *Love Does*. It portrays love as an action—an action that one can choose to engage in. I did a word study on 1 Corinthians 13 to help me make meaning of my call to the action of love: hospitality, xenia.

Poems/verses that remind me of God's truth:

Love is *patient*: the capacity to accept and tolerate delay, trouble, or suffering without getting angry or upset.

Love is *kind*: the quality of being friendly, generous, and considerate.

Love *rejoices in justice*: behaving according to what is morally right and fair; guided by truth, reason, justice, and fairness. But here's the deal: life isn't fair. So what I take this to mean is guided by truth, reason, and what we wish would be done unto us if the situation were reversed.

Love *rejoices in truth*: But what is truth? God's love is truth. His principles for life are full of truth. For me, this one is about inviting God into our thoughts so that our thoughts are transformed to be like His. My desire is to speak truth and ask God His opinion about my opinion in order to find truth. This truth is something we can rejoice in.

Love *never gives up*—love *perseveres*: Latin—to abide by something strictly, especially when it is *hard* to do; not giving up on someone. #StayAwayFromEasy #Integrity

> Love bears all things [regardless of what comes], believes all things [looking for the best in each one], hopes all things [remains steadfast during difficult times], endures all things [without weakening]. (1 Corinthians 13:7 AMP)

> For now . . . we have three things to do to lead us . . . trust steadily in God, hope unswervingly, love extravagantly, and the best of the three is love. (1 Corinthians 13:13 MSG)

Reflections through music and journaling:

Brandon Heath sings of this kind of love in "Love Never Fails." What do love and hospitality mean to you?

If love is an action, what can you do to show love to yourself today?

If love is an action, what can you do to show love to others today?

Closing prayer:

Thank you, Lord, for teaching me that it is equally important for me to practice love and hospitality for myself (see Matthew 22:39).

_____

_____

_____

_____

_____

_____

_____

_____

_____

_____

_____

Love is patient; love is kind.

Y IS FOR

YES

*Trust God from the bottom of your heart; don't try to
figure out everything on your own. Listen for God's voice
in everything you do, everywhere you go; he's the one who
will keep you on track.*
Proverbs 3:5–6 MSG

WHEN MY HEART WAS ON fire for the adventure of homeschool, I came across this in my devotional:

The Voice of Adventure:

There is a rawness and wonder to life. Pursue it. Hunt for it. Sell out to get it. Don't listen to the whines of those who settled for a second-rate life and want you to do the same so they won't feel guilty. Your goal is not to live long; it's to live. Jesus says the options are clear. On one side there is the voice of safety. You can build your fire in the hearth, stay inside, stay warm, dry and safe . . . or you can hear the voice of adventure—God's adventure. Instead, build a fire in your heart. Follow God's impulses. Adopt a child. Move overseas. Teach a class. Change careers. Run for office. Make a difference! Sure it isn't safe: but what is? (*Young Life Devotionals*)

There was a rawness and wonder I wanted to pursue. I didn't want to listen to the tugs of the world that tried to make me feel guilty. My goal was not to live large and busy—it was to live more freely and to enjoy the gift of my life with my husband and our five children. The options were clear to me. On one side there was the voice of safety—the safety of the familiar routine. On the other side was the voice of adventure—God's call to go to unfamiliar territory. #SayYesToAdventure!

As I mentioned earlier, people thought we were crazy for having five kids, let alone that we wanted to homeschool them. Can I just say, I have *zero* regrets in saying "Yes" to the adventure of having a large family. It has been such a rich blessing. God made me who I am, with my unique gifts. I continue to learn to trust Him that He will provide for me during challenging seasons of family life.

As our kids grow and leave the nest, it has been a delight to have them come home for Meier Monday dinners and for my favorite kitchen sign, GRAND CENTRAL STATION, to come to life!

I challenge you to wonder what saying "Yes" could lead to for you.

What I have learned about that:

When I seek adventures with God, sometimes I am challenged to say yes to waiting. I believe this kind of obedience can bring security and confidence that I talked about in "O Is for Obedience": that clear, peaceful feeling of knowing where I am supposed to be. I also gain wisdom as I practice gratitude during experiences that take me outside my comfort zone. #SayYes

Learning to say yes is life giving. Another adventure I learned to say yes to was when there wasn't much laughter in my life. I told you about how my dear Mr. Wonderful planned a surprise trip for us to see a comedy show. As I remember this experience, I want to maintain a posture of gratitude. It is an ongoing process for me as

I learn to receive God's love. I am getting better at recognizing how God loves me *through* my dear husband, my kids, and other people in my life. I continue to learn how to receive this love. #SayYes

Poems/verses that remind me of God's truth:

Wait: stay where one is or delay action until a particular time; to remain stationary in readiness, until the appointed time. I like the image of an athlete in "ready" position. This position makes it much easier to get where you need to go and is much more effective and efficient.

Say Yes

Accept His invitation! Say, Yes!
It could change Everything!
We need to cheer
the ones who are
dear in our lives.
Let's be clear,
fear never gets us
near our goal.

The life-giving Spirit of God will hover over (you), the spirit that brings wisdom and understanding, the Spirit that gives direction and builds strength, the Spirit that instills knowledge. (Isaiah 11:2 MSG)

Reflections through music and journaling:

I like the song, "Symphony" by Newsboys, for its reminder that if we aren't using the gifts God has given us or if we aren't accepting His invitation, we are wasting an opportunity.

What are you planning to do with this one precious life you've been given?

Look up the word *wait*. How does the definition inspire you? Challenge you?

How does the definition resonate as you process this verse?

> Wait on the Lord: be of good courage, and He shall strengthen your heart: wait, on the Lord. (See Psalm 27:14)

Closing prayer:

Thank You for guiding me along the adventures of life. Help me to keep saying yes to You and trusting You to lead me on my path toward authenticity.

_____

_____

_____

_____

_____

_____

_____

_____

_____

_____

_____

_____

_____

_____

_____

_____

_____

_____

_____

_____

_____

_____

_____

_____

_____

To avoid criticism: Say nothing, do nothing, be nothing!
—Aristotle

Z IS FOR

ZONE

No one will be able to stand up against you all the days of
your life . . . Have I not commanded you? Be strong and
courageous. Do not be terrified. Do not be discouraged,
for the Lord your God will be with you wherever you go.
Joshua 1:9 NIV

A FEW YEARS AGO, I SAW this plaque "Life Begins Just Outside Your Comfort Zone," and I realized that when I lean into the
discomfort of my anxious thoughts, the Lord will give me energy,
stamina, and strength to live into my calling. I have since learned
that whatever stage or season I am in, I can live the good life. Because if I'm honest, I am always just outside my comfort zone!

I've heard it said that the most useful knowledge about human
behavior is based on people's lived experiences. I hope that you have
received useful truths by hearing parts of my lived experiences. I've
done some hard work . . . I now realize I am living the dream . . .
my dream. God created me for my zany life of raising five kids. He
wired me with my unique set of strengths and gifts for my journey.

When I am outside my comfort zone, I need to remember the
words in "When the Crazy Kicks In" by Francesca Battestelli. In
every stage of growth in our family, I always have better days when

I pause before rushing into each new day. God promises to give me *all* I need to *do all* He wants me to do. So . . . I'd better get on the same page with God!

Z is also for Zeal: the great energy or enthusiasm gained in pursuit of a cause or an objective. In order for me to live my life with zeal, I need to embrace the fact that even when I am out of my comfort zone, God promises to take care of me.

I challenge you to start believing that living outside your comfort zone is part of God's plan for you.

Here is what I have learned about that:

Back in 2012 when my kids were sixteen, fourteen, twelve, nine, and seven, I felt trapped in a holding pattern and suffered a lack of zeal. I was a mess—a train wreck, actually.

When I am hit with train-wreck emotions, it usually happens because I forgot to start my day with seeking God first. Running on my own strength causes train-wreck emotions.

Poems/verses that remind me of God's truth:

TRAIN WRECK

Trapped Feelings
Running
Amuck
Inside Me! I desperately
Need a way to express them.
Wilting, Withering, Wanting to Run.
Ready to
Explode from lack of
Connection.
Keep the Faith, Keep the Faith!

ZEAL

Zestful
Effervescence;
Afraid of No one;
Limitless!

Light, space, zest—That's God! So with him on my side
I am fearless, afraid of no one and nothing. (Psalm 27:1
MSG)

Devote yourself to prayer, being watchful and thankful.
(Colossians 4:2 NIV)

Reflections through music and journaling:

"When the Crazy Kicks In" by Francesca Battestelli.
What do you do when the crazy kicks in during your day?
How do you re-center on crazy days?
Find out what you have been uniquely created to do. (See
StrengthFinders.com or take the iEQ9 individual inventory at
www.integrative9.com.)
Enjoy the adventure of becoming you!

Closing prayer:

Thank You that you will meet me in every moment if I pause to
invite You in. Help me to never forget that through the highs and
lows, I can redirect to see you directing me.

Life begins just outside your comfort zone.

The Lord bless you and keep you; the Lord make his face
shine on you and be gracious to you; the Lord turn his face
toward you and give you peace.
Numbers 6:24–26

DEAR LOVED ONE,

I have been on a learning path that has required some deep digging. I have made discoveries and have wrestled with many questions. I have come to realize that I have a strong need for connectedness: the energy that exists between people when they feel seen, heard, and valued; when they can give and receive without judgment; when they derive sustenance and strength from the relationship.

This is all personal and complex. The sum of what I have processed is that there are times when I do not feel connected to you, and that hurts my heart. I want to be connected, but I keep feeling let down, flattened, and disappointed by some of our interactions.

I believe countering my unforgiveness is a key component that will allow me to get closer to my goal of becoming the best possible version of myself. When I am aware of my need for healing, then I can forge ahead to use my healing story in an empowering way. I believe that wholeheartedness is part of God's plan for me (and for you.)

Here is what I have learned about that:

In order for me to reach my desired destination of wholeheart-edness, I realize that I need to come to a place of truth and forgive-ness. I do forgive you, and I believe that you never meant to hurt me. I believe that you have hurts of your own, and I continue to pray that you will find your own healing. I believe that on any giv-en day, it is quite possible that this letter could have been written by you.

Poems/verses to remind me of God's truth:

> *Grace is the reminder that we are all . . .*

God's
Redeemed and
Adored
Children for-
Ever

Reflections through music and journaling:

I trust that you can find your own way to forgiveness and the kind of grace described by Matthew West in "Grace Wins."

What if you were to write a letter back to me—what would you need to forgive me for?

Closing prayer:

Thank You, Lord, for your grace and forgiveness that gives me the power to have grace and forgiveness for others.

Grace Wins!

May grace and peace be with you. We have this hope as an
anchor for the soul, firm and secure.
Hebrews 6:19

⁙⁙⁙⁙⁙

DEAR SUFFERING ONE,

Our family loves to go to Disneyland. Actually, anything Disney gets us excited: we are in line the first day of a new release; we have vacationed to Disney destinations more times than we can count. Maybe it's because we have five kids with a ten-year age gap, or maybe it's because my husband and I are both young kids ourselves, or maybe it's just because we are young at heart.

Six years ago, we were introduced to a whole new side of Disney; we went to Dapper Day with my brother-in-law and sister-in-law. We went two or three more times with this new adult focus.

When my brother-in-law was diagnosed with cancer, he wanted to go one last time. The pace was definitely slower, with necessary wheelchair transfers, but that will always be one of our favorite trips. Kelly fully embraced his last trip to Disneyland. His first stop was to the Mad Hatter for a set of Mickey ears custom embroidered with "Brain Tumor Tour" on the back. We went on all his favorite rides, stopped at all the usual snack places, and had a special celebration dinner at Napa Rose with his favorite waiter, Rodney. This trip was in early November, so the park was decorated for Christmas. We cherish the picture in front of the giant tree on Main Street.

Here is what I have learned about that:

I realized that Kelly had a cancer that had a name and a diagnosis. However, I believe we all have a "cancer" in us that can only be addressed when we decide to let go of our agenda and invite God to have His way with us, to transform and heal us. (See "E Is for Empathy.")

Poems/verses to remind me of God's truth:

Brain Tumor Tour *(November 16–18, 2015)*

(We) spent the (last few days together) pretending nothing was wrong. It was a Pleasant Fiction and (we were) happy until we flew (home) and reality returned. Richard Paul Evans, *Mistletoe Inn*

Bonding and
Recognizing our
Affinity to have fun while wanting to
Ignore our
New reality.

Taking in
Unpredictable
Moments at favorite places—
Outstanding service from
Rodney, our favorite server@NapaRose.

Time
Of togetherness we will
Undeniably NEVER
REGRET

Reflections through music and journaling:

"Eye of the Storm" by Ryan Stevenson (featuring Gabe Real)
How do the lyrics of this song encourage you?
What if you shared this message with someone else today?
"When we share our greatest fears, our vulnerability, we bond in that honesty. We connect with each other and we don't feel so alone. And that's what [stories] are really about . . . connecting." (Richard Paul Evans, *Mistletoe Inn*)

Closing prayer:

Lord, thank You for people who have gone through storms before me, to share their stories and compassion with me.

When we share our vulnerability, we bond in that honesty.
—Richard Paul Evans

This world is led by the father of lies: God is
the Father of Light and Life.
See John 8:44

DEAR CHILDREN OF MINE,

This world is led by the father of lies; he would have you believe that something is wrong with you if you learn a certain way or look a certain way. God is the Father of light and life. He should be our go-to person in spiritual warfare. The father of lies is fighting to kill your soul. The Father of life is fighting for the life of your soul and spirit. He wants you to just be you, just as He created you to be—cherished and loved.

All of you push me to keep growing. You affirm a quote from Maya Angelou: "When we know better, we do better." Might I lend you some of my faith? I believe that when you lean fully into God's arms, He will pour out his favor and love on us.

Think of it. You're God's favorite. Let that sink into your thoughts. I encourage you to make the following proclamation fully yours and begin tapping into the favor you have in God.

You are blessed with unparalleled, unmerited favor from the Lord towards you: favor is a shield around you; you are growing in favor, with God and with people; you are favored everywhere you go . . . @home,@school,@

work, in relationships, and in your walk with God. You are favored in all that you do: doors of opportunity are opening for you. Blessings are attracted to you; increase upon increase will flow toward you. (Graham Cooke)

I believe encountering my doubts and insecurities is a key component that allows me to become the best version of myself. When I am aware of my need for healing, I can forge ahead to use that healing story in an empowering way. I challenge you to start believing that favor, healing, and abundance are part of God's plan for you.

I love you with all my heart,

Mom

Poems/verses to remind you of God's truth:

Let nothing prevent you from completing your training in favor; joyfully give yourself to becoming a wholehearted person.

FAVOR

Flowing with
Abundant
Victories; With
Obstacles
Reduced

Reflections through music and journaling:

I want "The Very Best" for all of you. I've heard it said, God will release His blessings on you in proportion to the character you allow Him to develop. As "This Is Your Life" to live, I pray that you will invite God into it and learn to "Thrive." (Song references by Francesca Battistelli, Switchfoot, and Casting Crowns.)

Your dad and I chose a life verse for each of you at your infant baptisms:

Proverbs 3:4–5 (NIV); Jeremiah 29:11; Colossians 3:12, 15; Isaiah 30:21; Proverbs 3:4–5 (MSG); Proverbs 18:10; Ephesians 6:10 (Living Bible); Numbers 6:24–26. I am regularly reminded that there is a message in each of these verses for me as well. Committing them to memory has helped me sense God's presence when I need Him the most.

Closing prayer:

Lord, thank You for the great privilege of being mom to five wonderful blessings.

When we know better, we do better. —Maya Angelou

Those who seek the Lord lack no good things.
Psalm 34:10 NIV

Dear Younger Me,

You will make mistakes in life and often wish you could have a chance to do certain parts over. My desire in writing this book was to share some of my mistakes and to encourage you. Dare to dream, know your strengths as well as your weaknesses, and do something every day that is life giving.

My sincere hope is for you to someday encourage others by sharing the lessons you have learned on your journey, that they may save your readers from some of the angst that you experienced. Remember to take in daily doses of encouragement and journal.

If you counter your regrets, you will grow into completeness. I challenge you to start to wonder what completeness might look like as part of God's plan for you. Who knows—maybe you will write a book someday.

With sincere encouragement,

Dana

Reflections through music and journaling:

"Fix Your Eyes" by For King & Country.

Go. Dare to dream. Start your journey to joy.

Closing prayer:

May the Lord bless and keep you; the Lord make his face shine on you and be gracious to you; . . . and give you peace. (Numbers 6:24–26 NIV)

Dare to dream.

FINAL THOUGHTS

THANK YOU FOR READING MY book.

Just because I have written this book doesn't mean I have it all figured out. My husband and I just started reading John Ortberg's book *If You Want to Walk on Water, Get Out of the Boat*. It's all about living outside your comfort zone and trusting Jesus to walk with you.

As I finish this book, I feel encouraged and excited. Encouraged that I got out of "my boat of fear and self-doubt" and wrote my story; excited to see what God will challenge me to do next.

As I end this adventure and wonder what is next, my goal is to continue living as Casting Crowns suggests in "Life Song." I want to praise the Lord with my daily worship and offer a living sacrifice to the One who wired me to do what I do.

Please feel free to email me questions, comments, or feedback as you continue on your journey.

Warmly,
Dana Meier
www.danameier.com

RESOURCES

Book references in order of appearance:

Introduction—Hatmaker, Jen, *Seven*. USA. BBooks, 2011.

Introduction—Brown, Brené, PhD, LMSW. *Rising Strong*. New York. Spiegel and Grau, 2015.

E Is for Empathy—Brown, Brené, PhD, LMSW. *Rising Strong*. New York. Spiegel and Grau, 2015.

H Is for Hope—Verde, Susan. *I am Love*. USA. Abrams Books, 2019.

Lamott, Anne. *Help, Thanks, WOW*. New York. Riverhead Books, 2012.

I Is for Integrity—Niequist, Shauna. *Present Over Perfect*. USA. Zondervan, 2016.

J Is for Joy—L'Engle, Madeleine. *A Wind in the Door*. USA. Farrar, Straus and Giroux, 1973.

K Is for Known—Vancil, Marilyn. *Self to Lose, Self to Find*. USA. Redemption Press, 2017.

O Is for Obedience—Freeman, Emily P., *The Next Right Thing*. Revell, 2015.

Dear Suffering One—Evans, Richard Paul. *Mistletoe Inn: A Novel*. Simon and Schuster, 2015.

Thank You—Ortberg, John. *If You Want to Walk on Water, Get Out of the Boat*. Grand Rapids, Michigan. Zondervan, 2001.

ABOUT THE AUTHOR

DANA MEIER, MED, "RETIRED" FROM teaching after eight years to raise her family. She is a professional home executive who has raised five children. She homeschooled for fifteen years and has been married for twenty-nine years. Dana lives in Seattle with her husband, Marv, and her two youngest children.
www.danameier.com

ORDER INFORMATION

To order additional copies of this book, please visit
www.redemption-press.com.
Also available on Amazon.com and BarnesandNoble.com
or by calling toll-free 1-844-2REDEEM.